Women's Writing

A CHALLENGE TO THEORY

Women's Writing

A CHALLENGE TO THEORY

EDITED BY
MOIRA MONTEITH
Lecturer in English Studies
Sheffield City Polytechnic

WITHDRAWN

HARVESTER PRESS · SUSSEX
ST. MARTIN'S PRESS · NEW YORK

First published in Great Britain in 1986 by
THE HARVESTER PRESS LIMITED
Publisher: John Spiers
16 Ship Street, Brighton, Sussex
and in the USA by
ST. MARTIN'S PRESS, INC.
175 Fifth Avenue, New York, NY 10010

British Library Cataloguing in Publication Data
Women's Writing: a challenge to theory.
   1. English literature — Women authors
   — History and criticism   2. English
   literature — 20th century — History
   and criticism
   I. Monteith, Moira
   820.9'9287   PR116

   ISBN 0-7108-0917-4

Library of Congress Cataloging-in-Publication Data
Women's Writing.
   Includes bibliographies and index.
   1. Women authors.   2. Literature — women authors —
history and criticism.   3. Feminist literary criticism.
   I. Monteith, Moira.
   PN471.W58   1986   809'.89287   86-10056
   ISBN 0-312 88798-1

Typeset in 11 on 12 point Baskerville

Printed in Great Britain

THE HARVESTER PUBLISHING PRESS GROUP
The Harvester Group comprises Harvester Press Ltd (chiefly
publishing literature, fiction, philosophy, psychology, and science and
trade books); Harvester Press Microform Publications Ltd (publishing
in microform previously unpublished archives, scarce printed sources,
and indexes to these collections) Wheatsheaf Books Ltd chiefly
publishing in economics, international politics, sociology, women's
studies and related social sciences); Certain Records Ltd, and John
Spiers Music Ltd (music publishing).

CONTENTS

CONTRIBUTORS

Linda Anderson is a lecturer in English Literature at the University of Newcastle upon Tyne. She has written a book on the Edwardian novel and is currently writing on Women and Autobiography (Harvester Press, forthcoming). She is one of the editors of *Writing Women*.

Shirley Foster is a lecturer in English Literature at the University of Sheffield. *Victorian Women's Fiction: Marriage, Freedom and the Individual* was published spring 1985 and she is currently researching for a book on Victorian women travellers. She is also contributing to *A Feminist Companion to Literature in English* (forthcoming, 1986/87).

Maggie Humm is currently Co-ordinator of Women's Studies at North-East London Polytechnic. Her PhD is in anarchist criticism and her research on women and education appears in *Women's Studies International Forum, Canadian Woman Studies* and *Towards the Community University* (ed. D. Teather, Kogan Page). She is now working on a book, *Feminist Criticism*, and compiling *An Annotated Biography of Feminist Criticism* (both Harvester Press).

Nicole Ward Jouve has published in French *Le Spectre du gris* (stories which she has translated as *Shades of Grey*, Virago); *L'Entremise* (a novel); and *Un homme nommé Zapolski* (which she has rewritten as *The Streetcleaner: an Essay on the Yorkshire Ripper Case*, Marion Boyars, 1985). All three at the Editions des femmes; in barely mitigated English: *Baudelaire, a Fire to Conquer Darkness* (Macmillan, 1980); and a number of articles, the one she likes best being 'From Mud to the Void: *The Children of Violence*', in J. Taylor, *Notebooks, Memoirs, Archives: Reading and Re-Reading Doris Lessing*. She is currently working on a book on *Colette* (Harvester Press).

She insists that Ward Jouve (no hyphen) does not constitute a double-barrel name. She says that the English and the French surnames are like two webs for 'Nicole' to waddle or paddle on on ordinary days, but that (as with James Bond's vehicles) they can double up as wings on good days.

Moira Monteith is a lecturer in the English Studies Department at Sheffield City Polytechnic. She has published articles on Marge Piercy, Ursula Le Guin and Doris Lessing as well as editing the British edition of the *Hemingway Review*. She is currently researching the use of computers in English Studies.

Sue Roe is the author of a novel, *Estella, Her Expectations* (Harvester, 1982; paperback 1983). Her critical study, *Writing and Gender: Virginia Woolf's Writing Practice* is published by Harvester (1986). Five of her poems appeared in Spring 1986 in *PEN New Poetry 1* ed. Robert Nye (Quartet). She is now completing a second novel.

Lorna Sage teaches at the University of East Anglia, where she is currently Dean of the School of English and American Studies. She has written on Milton, on Meredith, and on various contemporary women novelists.

Marian Shaw is a lecturer in English at the University of Hull. She is currently writing a book on Winifred Holtby and also writing on Tennyson on whom she has published in the past.

Emma Tennant grew up in Scotland, and worked as a freelance journalist before editing the literary newspaper *Bananas* and then full-time novel writing. Her most recent novel is *Black Marina* (Faber and Faber, 1985).

Michelene Wandor is a poet, playwright and critic. She was poetry editor and a regular theatre reviewer for *Time Out* magazine (1971-82). She writes extensively for theatre and radio, some of her recent work for the latter includes a feature on Jean Rhys, and an eight-part dramatisation of Dostoyevsky's *The Brothers Karamazov*. Her recent publications include *On Gender and Writing* (Pandora Press), *Five Plays* (Playbooks/Journeyman) and *Gardens of Eden: poems for Eve and Lilith* (Playbooks/Journeyman). A collection of stories, *Guests in the Body* is published in early 1986.

INTRODUCTION

Moira Monteith

... my concern lies in the other, what is heterogeneous, my own negation erected as representation, but the consumption of which I can also
decipher. (Julia Kristéva) [1]

One of the immense positive gains accruing from feminist
criticism has been the realisation that the female in literature is
a literary construct. That may seem a very obvious statement.
Didn't we always know that everything in literature is constructed? At one level, yes. But the act of construction didn't
seem to matter very much as long as it was considered in terms of
craftsmanship. (The gender implicit in the word is entirely
relevant here.) Traditionally, there has always been a general
assumption that the better the craftsman the less visible the
structural details. The literary work should be like a seamless
robe knitted on one needle, indicating the aesthetic impossibility of separating form from content.

Virginia Woolf called this quality 'integrity'. To achieve such
integrity writers must have minds which have 'consumed all
impediments'.[2] A writer who is also an underprivileged person
is liable to reveal awkwardnesses which arise from an over-
whelming sense of unfairness and intrude into the fabric of the
work. She instances Charlotte Brontë who 'left her story, to
which her entire devotion was due to attend to some personal
grievance'.[3] Woolf considered that as long as most women
writers were also underprivileged people, as valued in terms of
their own society, their work was and is bound to suffer. Some
women were able to overcome this disability – she thought Jane
Austen an exception to the rule.

1

More recent feminist critics have shown that the absence of much female experience from literature, the narrowness of depiction, the obsessive repetition of a few acceptable roles, can be seen as overall structural defects in any author's work just as much as the intrusion of 'some personal grievance'. Such criticism refuses to accept a literary work as 'seamless', and collaborates with a post-structural approach in separating the signifier from the signified. This splitting of the components of literature has released new critical energy, in which feminist approaches are of fundamental importance. There is a good argument for beginning any course in literary criticism with a foundation of feminist criticism, since such an approach signifies the essential nature of literary construction.

For several decades now feminist critics have spent time and words revealing the distortion of female experience in literature. Images of power when related to women are also images of fear. The range of female characterisation is extremely narrow: seductive creature, domestic angel, victim, mother, witch or prophet. Often such roles overlap and often moral consider-ations external to the needs of the text are involved. A mother who is a 'good' mother is usually only indirectly connected with power if at all, whereas seductiveness can be viewed as powerful since it is related to instinctual urges which may disrupt the smooth face of patriarchy.

Such distortion, because so obviously a construct, contradicts any theory of art based on realistic presentation. Nevertheless realism (or its predecessor, a selective imitation of nature) is still remarkably resilient. We often seem tied to the notion of realistic presentation as if the umbilical cord between fiction and what we think of as reality must never be cut. Some critics who have delineated scrupulously the narrow (and therefore distorted) presentation of women have overlooked the nature of literature as construct and instead called for a wider, stronger, more positive range of characterisation. 'There is a female voice that has rarely spoken for itself in the English novel – the voice of the shopgirl and the charwoman, the housewife and the barmaid.'[4] Presumably, they would not be speaking as authors or creators but giving us the authenticity of their own experience.

A theory or practice of writing based on realism has an

2

indirectly sinister (and in the long run, debilitating) effect: it denies the real forces that go into the making of literature, the social and psychological pressures that function alongside the craft of the individual writer. If these pressures become obvious the value of the work diminishes in due measure, is considered to be insufficiently 'crafted'. Correspondingly, the lack of critical awareness (or its suppression) often means that we fail to note specific tensions, contradictions and gaps within a literary work unless the race, class, sect or gender stereotypes are unbelievably crass. A continual regard for something akin to Woolf's 'integrity' has led to a continuing and widening estrangement for women writers when faced with the models of 'great' literature. Inevitably there has been a call for different models and a re-examination of language use.

Feminist criticism, like a solar oven, has proved to be the mirror that focuses literature and concentrates its signifying energy. In accomplishing this it has also made clear that despite all claims to the contrary, criticism is in one particular the same as any construct: it is part of its time and environment. Critics are subject to social and psychological pressures in the same way writers are.

Given that criticism is a construct which is affected by several pressures including that of gender, it follows that research interests also will reveal the effects of those forces. Certain areas have been left relatively unexplored, mainly because they were not considered important in terms of prevailing critical opinion. One such neglected area has been the process of creativity as it concerns women writers. We need to recognise the legitimate connections between the environment in which a work is created and the finished product and the specific factors that affect women; to explore the relationship between creativity and criticism noting particularly the constraints imposed by any literary canon; and to understand the sense of alienation that some writers experience when they try to use the medium of language that superficially appears free for all.

The last decade has seen increasing research and comment on such topics. A new consideration of the relationship between creativity and criticism (particularly as both relate to the use of language) could have an equally positive and salutary effect as the work done previously on images of women in literature and the examination of male-dominated or phallocentric criticism.

While that is so, it is also the case that an unproven and largely unresearched opposition between the role of critic and that of writer has been taken for granted. Many critics have asserted quite reasonably that their profession is also creative but the qualities traditionally valued as integral to literary criticism – intelligent appraisal, rational evaluation, objective judgement – are not those normally associated with writers as artists. Indeed, they are normally associated with masculine values and experiences. This may be why so many male critics have been drawn to the notion of a 'science' of literary criticism and latch on to analytic procedures such as structuralism. Whereas subjectivity, personal involvement and the apparently non-rational element of inspiration are often associated with female experience in general as well as with writers of both sexes. The two axes, male/female, critical/creative, intersect in popular imagination as well as in literary critical discourse and inevitably give rise to problems of definition.

Ubiquitous metaphors of pregnancy (the birth of new books, concepts, stylistic devices) indicate the connection often made between the female role and literary creativity, even though such metaphors are frequently used by and about male writers. The ambivalence in the use of such terminology indicates our general confusion. Understandably, male appropriation of creativity does seek to use specific gender terms. For instance, male writers and critics can be described as 'seminal', a word which negates any feminine associations and implies both a sense of power and the establishment of a tradition. The seeds of such a tradition can be counted in two ways: as the scions of a patrimony carrying on the line from generation to generation or, following Harold Bloom, the rejection by the sons of the literary practices and objectives of their predecessors. Either way the line is predominantly male with a few aberrant females. The confusing nature of such terminology is obvious in the case of a writer such as Mary Shelley. She has been hailed as the mother of an entirely new genre,[5] science fiction (ironically for a book concerned with the horror of birth without subsequent nurture, creation without consideration), but the 'seminal' effect of *Frankenstein* is undeniable.

The problem of gender association and the values we as a

4

society give to qualities considered as masculine or feminine may go some way to explain why Virginia Woolf considered androgyny a desirable condition for writers. And why the debate on androgyny continues still. Woolf realised the importance of gender to the act of writing as perhaps no one previously had done and her plea for writers to have both male and female qualities has been widely discussed in relation to her own work, and often repudiated or explained away apologetically by feminist critics. Certainly, very few commentators seem to embrace her notion of androgyny at all enthusiastically. Woolf wrote both novels and criticism and the two activities are constantly separated in critical comment on her work. Her desire for 'integrity', for a holistic approach, is entirely understandable. The concept of wholeness, of completion, is highly attractive in itself, presumably because of the social value we give to it. In terms of critical definition, a writer may seek to avoid classification on partial grounds, gender being notoriously partial. The desire of some women writers not to be seen as 'women writers' is long established. The learned characteristics of masculinity or femininity always co-exist to some extent in any individual. Perhaps Woolf is commenting on the creative force brought into being by the juxtaposition of such qualities rather than an amorphous combination.

Intertextuality is a concept which seems particularly important and relevant to women at the moment, both as writers and as critics. It is noticeable how many of the contributors to this book are concerned with the theory and practice of re-writing, of pulling a text out of a previous text, of fighting for a location on ground already occupied by other 'jargons' or varieties of language, of creating a place in language where different voices could be heard. I believe that social values encoded in the text at the time of writing are also part of its intertextuality and those specifically applying to gender differences are particularly relevant to the feminist critic. The notion of what both writer and reader bring to the text is increasingly important. As writers, critics and readers we function on at least two levels, with simultaneous conscious and unconscious motivations.

Therefore we can afford to be more positive about fragmentation and division. This book is a collection of fragments where the juxtaposition, the edging is important. All the papers are concerned with the relationship of female experience to the process of writing. The contributions do not follow one coherent design (nor were intended to do so) nor speak with one voice, yet none is without parallel points of interest in the papers of other contributors. They can be viewed as a collection by analogy with women's discussion, a model of collaboration rather than one of antithetical argument.[6]

The activity of writing is apparently open to everyone, and given a reasonable level of literacy in a society this is to some extent true. After all, Jane Austen and many like her could and did write in the drawing-room at home. Class and income obviously have a great deal to do with the leisure and confidence available for writing, but even so the world of the book would seem open for all to explore. In the first paper, Lorna Sage pertinently considers what some women writers have done to claim that world. She looks at it as a space defined by relationships. What is at first seen as a place for a love affair is defined finally as a battleground. Writers fight to gain a place for their view, their transposition of experience. There is no empty place waiting to be settled, no vacuum waiting to be filled.

Sage first of all writes about women who for a long time didn't secure much of a place within that world, Rhys, Stead and Smart. Yet all desired to appropriate something from female experience to alter the world of the text and to parody or examine the problems of gender in the world in which they lived. She quotes Rhys's powerful image of marginalisation, where women are quite literally written into the margin by the comments a male reader writes in his copy of a book. Sage claims that in their later work these writers colluded with their marginality and wrote this experience into the text.

Since it is possible to see the world of writing as open and accessible to anyone, it is therefore tempting to see the author as androgynous. Sage doesn't find such a proposition intellectually appealing, believing as she does that the concept is platonic and based on homosexuality. No sex difference is involved therefore and the concentration on masculinity is perpetuated in the reception of women's writing and the canon in which they usually fail to find a niche. Such a process of legitimation may explain the success of women writers who have chosen to write in the alternative dimension of Gothic. Significantly, as Sage points out, feminist critics have begun to redistribute textual space.

Sage concludes her conceptually vigorous argument by concentrating on one writer. She exploits her previous knowledge and work on Doris Lessing to come to a definitive statement about Lessing's use of space. Using Barthes's definition of atopia, the location of texts within the world of language, where jargon fights with jargon for privilege and priority, she finds Lessing articulating now from the position where she began. Barthes's statement that 'language comes from some place' indicates that Lessing is still colonial, still dissident. She exemplifies the position of the explorative writer: the territory is already settled, her words must fight for their place.

Nicole Ward Jouve makes her bilingualism the starting place from which she examines her own writing practice. Her presence in one country or language means her absence in another so she has no 'contemporary' French nor any long-felt associations with concepts she finds peculiarly English. She has come to see that her two languages could be viewed as maternal and paternal and that (following Cixous and Kristéva) French was for her (and perhaps is) pre-Oedipal, 'of the body', while English functions as a patriarchal, symbolic, law-giving language. It seems indicative that she has written most of her fiction in French, most of her criticism in English.

The two languages result in one obvious form of dual identification but the sense of a double exists for Jouve on a number of levels. It is more complex than outright identification with another facet of self. She finds links between a writer's individual thoughts and creation, and experiences unknown to the writer which are happening to other people. The secrecy, the privacy of writing may be more impersonal, more public, more widely interpretable than it is normally considered to be. Women may find it particularly difficult to bring such connections to light since self-censorship is a peculiarly strong pressure on them, controlled as they often are by family conventions about 'outside' behaviour.

Jouve is not so much concerned with giving a voice to characters previously unrepresented in fiction (for example, the prostitute victims of a murderer) as to create an area of language where such a voice might be heard. The subtle distinction

7

between broader realistic portrayal, that is widening the range of characters that appear in realist texts, and expanding the accepted conventions of discourse is highly relevant here.

The act of translating from the words of one language to another or from one experience into another, reduces the sense of an 'authoritative' version. Jouve suggests that the activity might be considered as peculiarly female. Her own inimitable use of language is a marvellously multi-layered combination of the unconscious and the conscious, so that the ambiguities of a phrase such as 'water over the bridge' can only be appreciated fully in terms of two languages, two cultures.

She also maintains that a sense of displacement or strain is inevitable for anyone in a dual or bilingual situation. She seems to be saying implicitly in this paper that meaning is conveyed by difference, our experience is never totally definable but always relative. She names herself moitié-de-poulet, half of one thing, half of another. But half is less than one if viewed from a single, defining viewpoint, but also, and conversely, two halves are in many ways larger than one.

Linda Anderson's important paper considers the construction of a fictional self for women and the rewriting of their experiences, the need for secrecy and the desire for openness. She looks at the relationship between women's autobiography and their apprehension of a sexual identity, and the defining of 'self'. Memories, suppressed or consciously brought to mind, are significantly related to the sex of the rememberer and she examines Freud's statements from this viewpoint.

It has proved difficult for women to publish their own experiences openly, so the diary has been a very important means of expression. Even published writers such as Virginia Woolf found the form of the diary liberating or exploratory, a place where things could be written that were not written either in letters or published work. Kate Millett who did publish her own experiences apologised for her lack of good taste, for transgressing the social codes. The necessity for secrecy has been an important factor, first of all in what women felt able to express, and secondly in what was considered publishable.

Anderson states that women writing about themselves are producing fictional constructs which inevitably are affected by the writers' inscription within a sexual code. Nevertheless, they are also writing about what others have written or said about women and so are in the process of re-writing. She comments on the 'silent and unrecorded areas of experience', areas that have never been dealt with in print and the important and creative act of fictionalising gaps in history and tradition: for example Woolf's creation of Shakespeare's sister.

Michelene Wandor is both a theoretical writer (mainly in her political, feminist work but also some literary criticism) and a creative writer. She skilfully uses this dichotomy to involve us in reading her own work while at the same time viewing it critically. The poems are juxtaposed with analysis both of the writing as text and the process of its creation. She considers the nature of the political voice, how it made itself felt in her work, and its conjunction with theory. We then experience the effect of that theoretical impact on the form of a poem, where the poem has symbolic spaces and unfinished lines and fragmentary statements. Like Nicole Jouve she uses the word 'schizophrenia' to describe a particular experience as a writer. She found she wrote personally in poetry and plays, politically in journalism though subsequently this distinction altered. She is curious about the ways in which poetry tries to deal with emotion and ideas at the same time, where the different voices of poetic and political discourse come together. There is an apparent conflict between the rationality of theory and political writing and the wildness, the relative unpredictability of a poem. Her own sense of dislocation seems threefold: woman, Jew, feminist, three 'margin voices' from exile. It is interesting to note how she can lay claim quite justifiably to the Old Testament as a Jew whereas it does seem very difficult to claim it as a woman.

I have written 'feminist criticism' in previous paragraphs and probably gave the impression of a discrete scholarly approach. But Maggie Humm unerringly reveals how feminist criticism is itself institutionalised within specific practices. She starts from the premise that nationalist division detracts from the viability or forcefulness of the attack against the universality of patriarchy; and that feminist criticism would benefit from a combination of the American and English approaches. Her account of the critical procedures followed in England and America by feminist critics makes clear that there is no single methodology. The observable differences appear to follow lines already laid down in national practice. Feminist criticism (as any other critical approach) has reacted to the particular methodologies dominant in either America or England.

American feminist critics in her opinion have tended mainly to work within academic channels but accompanying that approach have valorised women's experience in areas of traditional skills and knowledge which previously went unrecognised. They have broadened the acceptance of new literary material, notably works by black, lesbian and ethnic writers. English feminist critics have positioned literary criticism within a more general cultural discussion and have politicised their practice to a much greater extent. Discussion and research on literature has been widened considerably as a result of both approaches though the practice of literary criticism has changed far less than has the literary canon.

Humm considers that archaeology (recovery of previous women writers who had been 'undiscovered' or whose reputations had been neglected or unreasonably declined) came first and that theoretical work subsequently developed from that basis. However, if this is so, and historically it does seem so, notions of critical theory must have informed the work of the archaeologists/recoverers as otherwise how would they have developed national biases?

The paper focuses on the work of a number of critics from the 1970s onwards and several critical approaches since neither nation has a monolithic school of literary criticism. Humm compares in some detail American and English approaches to reader-response theory and their differing views as to what constitutes difference. Some American critics have looked for specific American referrents; for example, their concept of outsiders, the wilderness, oral traditions. It may be that such critical data could be relevant to the literature of other countries if concepts relating to practices elsewhere could be seen to be similar in kind.

In England feminist criticism has been tempered by the fact that feminists are more likely to look to cultural critics such as Althusser to explain systems of oppression. They have therefore been less interested in a wide recovery of female writers since not everything written by women is deemed feminist.

Criticism does arise from a social and historical context so it is understandable how national approaches have been reinforced. It would seem from Humm's paper that feminist criticism is still reactive rather than pro-active. Undoubtedly she has drawn our attention to a crisis point as regards the future development of feminist criticism: its relationship with other critical and cultural theories.

Emma Tennant and Sue Roe engage at several points with matters that other writers in this collection have touched on quite independently: for example, the author's sense of dislocation, the emergence of the double in writing, the dishonesty of the writer herself. Perhaps, as Nicole Jouve writes, 'the famous *zeitgeist*; or Doris Lessing's concentric circles, what she calls "ripples from the storm": the same "fads", mysteriously carried by atmospheric mental waves, reach a wide range of apparently disconnected people.'

We have retained the form of the discussion as far as possible and tried not to rewrite it as a formal discourse, since the spontaneous nature of the discussion gives it a particular intensity and encourages a more wide-ranging approach than could have occurred within a formally written account. We also wanted to keep the collaborative nature of the dialogue, its reverberations and ricochets, even to the point of one person finishing another's sentence.

Emma Tennant spells out the selfconsciousness of a woman who is a writer and sympathetically aware of the women's movement, and yet has used extremist feminism as an equivalent of Calvinist repression. Her own sense of the double - a feature in much of her writing - may have come from the dislocation between her first years and later life, in terms of language and consciousness. Her awareness of the power relationship between male and female has affected the structure of some of her novels, so that the kernel is concerned with female characters but is circumscribed by the male voice of authority. In one of her most recent novels, *Woman Beware Woman*, she uses the device of a male figure absent from the action yet still the focus, dividing and ruling the women. Her realisation of male power and the female mixture of powerlessness and rationality which she finds difficult to convey, perhaps parallels her own childhood fears about identity.

Sue Roe reveals how her novel *Estella* is in some ways more feminist than she had thought at the time of writing. She is concerned with myth and personal myth and the immense importance this has to women who are featureless in terms of written history. As characters they exist somewhere between the archetype and the stereotype, for example Miss Havisham, 'the bride on ice'.

The discussion also focuses on the notion of writers such as Emma Tennant and Sue Roe, and previous novelists such as Virginia Woolf and Jean Rhys pulling a new story out of an existing one, and so leads on to the influence of literary texts and the question of rewriting what has gone before.

In their comparative studies of women's writing Shirley Foster and Marion Shaw look respectively at what was happening during the early twentieth century in America and between the wars in England. Reading the two papers in conjunction is exceedingly interesting since the theory Shaw puts forward concerning women writers' dichotomy of approach could be exemplified in Foster's textual analysis. Foster considers three books written by Wharton, Chopin and Cather, published between 1899 and 1915, and finds evidence of ambivalence in all three writers concerning woman's status, role and opportunities. She starts from the premise that:

> artistic as well as social ideologies have prevented women novelists in particular from articulating openly their own dissent from accepted notions of female roles, especially those concerning the sacredness of marriage and motherhood; in order to formulate their protest, they have had to implement strategies of deviousness, using artistic devices which voice their unease without obviously challenging literary or sexual conventions.

Even the most innovative novel of the three, Chopin's *The Awakening*, is resolved only by the heroine's suicide.

The three novels discussed are not experimental in form but all challenge traditional assumptions about the presentation of a heroine and her aspirations. Foster examines perceptively and carefully the effects of imagery and other patterning devices. She concludes that all three writers resist falsifying sexual ideologies. The inevitable ambivalence must surely indicate a particular stage in the rejection of traditional assumptions.

Shaw looks at writers whom she believes no longer had 'to

write like a man ... to be taken seriously'. They were self-consciously aware of their position as writers and debated the possibility then as now as to whether their writing should be distinct from established literary practice. She demonstrates how writers tended to take two different directions even though the philosophy of feminism overlapped both approaches. The more experimental writers, such as Dorothy Richardson, Jean Rhys and Rosamund Lehmann seem 'invariably pessimistic in [their] depiction of heroines who are vulnerable, dependent, forsaken and self-absorbed.' Whereas writers such as Phyllis Bentley, Naomi Mitchison and Winifred Holtby carried on the realist tradition but illustrated women's lives in detail in ways neglected by male Edwardian writers. They also spent much time and energy in writing very detailed and well-documented historical novels, thus claiming some part in history for women absent from orthodox history.

Shaw uses Holtby in particular to show this dichotomy of direction, in that she wrote in the realist tradition with 'positive' heroines yet was sufficiently interested in Virginia Woolf to write a critical account of her work. Holtby defines Woolf's 'two streams of thought' as 'one practical, controversial, analytical; the other creative, poetical, audacious, – a distinctly polarised division of terms.

In this paper Shaw illustrates clearly the parameters of the discussion about women's writing as it was debated between the wars. It is evident from the other papers that the discussion is by no means finished although its grounds are slightly different.

The work of a writer exists as a part of the historical process and yet simultaneously encodes history within itself. It can be separated by time and space from its genesis, and then the authority of the author declines to a kind of radioactive half-life whereas that of the critic apparently increases, having to do with the response, reception, relationship, recovery of texts. Certainly many writers and critics are much more conscious now of the variety of relationships existing within the text and surrounding its production and reception. Some writers are deliberately creating 'open' texts which by their structure invite more than one reading, more than one interpretation. Take for instance Angela Carter's statement: 'I try, when I write fiction, to think on my feet – to present a number of propositions in a variety of different ways, and to leave the reader to construct her own fiction for herself from the elements of my fictions.'[7] This new consciousness on the part of the writer, coupled with our acceptance of the fragmentary nature of the text, involves a more sophisticated response from the reader. It seems less and less likely that writers will now aim for 'integrity', androgynous or not.

The innovative nature of feminist criticism will continue in all probability for some time to come but the relationship between it and the writing of literature will remain, at least for the time being, conjectural. Undoubtedly women writers feel moved to respond to the pressures generated by feminist criticism (even if the response is a rejection) in a way that previous writers as a group have never felt so called upon. The effects of those pressures and how they interact with other social or psychological pressures on the individual writer and with the kind of stimulus arising from theory Micheline Wandor writes about have yet to be deciphered.

The links between writing, feminist criticism and women's creativity have been considered through a number of approaches in this collection. Read it as you will.

Notes

1. Julia Kristéva (1974), 'The Novel as Polylogue', *Desire in Language,* ed. Leon Roudiez, trans. T. Gora, A. Jardine and L. Roudiez (Basil Blackwell, Oxford, 1980) p. 163.
2. Virginia Woolf (1929), *A Room of One's Own* (The Hogarth Press, London, 1967), p. 101.
3. *Ibid.*, p. 110.
4. Elaine Showalter, *A Literature of Their Own* (Virago, London, 1978), p. 314.
5. Robert Scholes and Eric Rabkin, *Science Fiction: History, Science, Vision* (Oxford University Press, 1977), p. 91.
6. In a recent seminar at Sheffield City Polytechnic, Cheris Kramerae discussed American feminist research into language use, and the apparent differences between male and female public discussion. Apparently women tend to be more collaborative in their approach than men.
7. Angela Carter, 'Notes from the Front Line', *On Gender and Writing*, ed. Michelene Wandor (Pandora Press, London, 1983), p. 69. The title of the article gives some reinforcement to Lorna Sage's definition of the place of writing as a battleground.

1

THE AVAILABLE SPACE

Lorna Sage

The Available Space

This piece is a very partial account of some women writers' relations to literary history, from two rather different points of view – first from the now familiar angle of exclusion; and secondly, in relation to notions of writing as (possibly) free space. I've taken a new look at the 'androgynous' model of creativity, and (in Doris Lessing's *Canopus* series) at a version of writing as no man's land. I've chosen the metaphor of 'space' because it seems to focus several issues at once – the 'autonomy' of the text; the vexed question of separate traditions; and the utopian (or atopian) impulse in women's writing. Also because it points to a fundamental literary paradox, neatly exemplified in the hopeful blurb of the recent *Chatto Book of Post-Feminist Poetry*: 'At least within the circumscribed world of the poems, they are fully liberated.' This notion of the 'world' on the page is an enduring critical myth that feminist thinking has again and again (and rightly) called in question. It is also, however, the reflex of a practical hope – that writing can test out and change the parameters of freedom.

I start from what Adrienne Rich calls 'The phantom of the man-who-would-understand, the lost brother, the twin –' and (with Lessing) go on to look at a reluctant and paradoxical version of the woman author *in authority*.

The Love Affair with Literature

> The typewriter is guilty with love and flowery with shame, and to me it speaks so loudly I fear it will communicate its indecency to casual visitors. (Elizabeth Smart, *By Grand Central Station I Sat Down and Wept*, 1945)

'The people I loved,' Christina Stead reminisced in 1981, at the age of seventy-nine, 'were Shelley and Shakespeare.'[1] She was thinking back to her Australian adolescence, and the way she was cut off from the patterns an orderly education and an orderly family life impose. Her novels of childhood and adolescence (*The Man Who Loved Children*, 1940; *For Love Alone*, 1944) have heroines who lead a secret, rebellious life through books. Teresa (*For Love Alone*) hasn't much of a bottom drawer; what she does have is an outrageous mental inventory, a library of transgressions in her head:

> Teresa knew all the disorderly loves of Ovid, the cruel luxury of Petronius, the exorbitance of Aretino, the meaning of the witches' Sabbaths, the experiments of Sade, the unimaginable horrors of the Inquisition, the bestiality in the Bible, the bitter jokes of Aristophanes and what the sex-psychologists had written . . .[2]

There are two love affairs in *For Love Alone* - one of them a love affair with writing. The pleasure of the text is an open book to Teresa, you might suppose. But no, not exactly, of course, because the happy promiscuity of print - the way books are 'anybody's' - is belied at the outset by the signatures on their title pages: 'her world existed and was recognised by men. But why not by women? She found nothing in the few works by women she could find that was what they must have felt.'[3] The old story: if Teresa had been able to afford to go to university, if she hadn't been antipodean and an autodidact, she'd doubtless have found a more moderate way of relating to a more suitable reading list, and it would have taken her longer to spot the anomaly in the situation of the literary groupie. As it is, she is destined to live through a kind of one-woman replay of the imaginative repertoire - Odyssey, medieval romance, folk-tale, fairy-tale - before her desires come into their own.

As for her author's desires, well, she was writing into a curious void. The history of the neglect of Stead's work (un-Australian, un-American, un-British as well as un-realistic) is well known, though it is worth reminding oneself that it had some special twists, that she was famous for being neglected, a *recognised* anomaly from (at least) 1940 on. She was the Emily Brontë *de leurs jours*, the classic outside the canon. There are many others in roughly the same tiresome category, and their careers provide a painful commentary on the love affair with letters. There is Jean Rhys, of course, who came back from the literary dead with *Wide Sargasso Sea* in 1966 only to confirm her strangeness. Looking back to her (West Indian) girlhood, in 1979, she wrote, 'As soon as I could I lost myself in the immense world of books, and tried to blot out the real world which was so puzzling to me.'[4] Elizabeth Smart's *By Grand Central Station* is a mosaic of quotations ('I am still empress of a new-found land, that neither Columbus nor Cortez could have equalled'[5]) and a much republished book (rediscovered last in 1977). My epigraph about the blushing typewriter comes from a section about 'collaborating' with her lover's writing while conspiring to break his marriage. The only women writers who figure at all prominently in the elaborate tissue of allusion are St Teresa of Avila and Emily Brontë: 'Heathcliff's look bored a hole through England which generations of heather on the wild moor have never erased.'[6]

There are lots of things that might be said about literariness, pastiche, allusion – connections, for example, with Ann Radcliffe, and the Gothic – but what I want to point to is the way the 'world' of books acts as a meeting-place. Stead's Teresa dreams of the university she never went to as an academy of love, where the young learn and elaborate the languages of passion:

> a gleaming meadow, in which beautiful youths and girls strolled, untangling intellectual and moral threads, but joyfully, poignantly, and weaving them together, into a moving, living tapestry, something into which love, the mind, the soul, and living beauties like living butterflies and early summer flower-knots were blended.[7]

Teresa's ordeal begins from her perverse refusal to give up this pleasurable space and accept sensuous illiteracy as her lot. As

I've argued elsewhere, *For Love Alone*, with its 'young woman's entrance into the world' plot, reads now like a novel about beginning *again* (Stead was in her forties) and a rejection of rejection. The 'enemy' (and this goes for Smart and Rhys too) is the destructive poverty and banality of what is constructed as the 'real' and the 'representative'. This is not, as I see it, an argument about 'fantasy' as a deviant genre, but about writing as a place in which sex-roles, for example, can be studied, appropriated, parodied, rather than taken for granted. To put it another way, these are writers who both play on gender difference and insist on sharing the 'same' territory. The reviewer who described *For Love Alone* as 'an Australian *Sons and Lovers* with a feminine Paul Morel'[8] was registering this in a backhanded fashion.

More straightforwardly, of course, what he implied was that the (British, male) tradition wasn't to be significantly rewritten this way. To treat male writers (and characters) as symbolic objects has always seemed anomalous, part of the 'Nellie, I am Heathcliff' syndrome. In short, a pigeonhole awaits. Much of Stead's and Rhys's later work (and Smart's companion piece to *By Grand Central Station*: *The Assumption of the Rogues and Rascals*, 1978) is about the process by which outsiders come to *represent* outsiders, and collude in not their exclusion, but (more horribly) their inclusion, madwomen with an attic apiece. A quotation from Smart:

> I raise my eyes to the books and say, Well *they* were here and whirl around still all over the western world, which means that their followers-on must too, for nothing stops so suddenly. Are they hidden in veils, or strait-jacketed by domestic lives or hammering at their sores in lonely rooms?[9]

Rhetorical questions set the keynote when Smart returns to writing, more than thirty years on: 'Is ego a prick to the Muse then?'[10] If the earlier novel celebrated archetypal euphoria and despair, this one speaks of tribulations for which the archetypes are missing: writing *at all* becomes the guiding obsession. And then, 'What if nobody listens?'[11]

The 'world of books' is one thing to the (female) reader, quite another to the writer who wants to write herself in between (across?) the lines. Jean Rhys has a story, 'The Insect World', set in London during the war, and published in *Sleep It Off Lady* (1976) which shows even the reader's refuge ('I lost myself in the immense world of books') under attack. Audrey is reading a second-hand novel which has inane comments from a previous reader pencilled in the margin:

> But it was on page 166 that Audrey had a shock. He had written 'Women are an unspeakable abomination' with such force that the pencil had driven through the paper ... And yet, she told herself, 'I bet if you met that man he would be awfully ordinary, just like everybody else.' It was something about his small, neat, precise handwriting that made her think so.[12]

Here the specifically sexual rejections and humiliations that shape Rhys's plots have surfaced on the page. Reading/writing become the site of exposure and shame (the other reader as flasher), and intimidation. In a story called 'The Lotus' (1967), the would-be woman writer is incarnated as Lotus Heath, middle-aged, over-painted, alcoholic and 'creative', who is introduced through the hostile speculations of her neighbours:

> 'Garland says she's a tart.'
> 'A tart! My dear Christine, have you seen her? After all, there are limits.'
> 'What, round about the Portobello Road? I very much doubt it.'
> 'Nonsense,' Ronnie said. 'She's writing a novel. Yes, dearie –' he opened his eyes very wide and turned the corners of his mouth down '– all about a girl who gets seduced –'[13]

When Lotus breaks down, tears her clothes off and runs into the street, the 'camp-follower' version of the relation between women and writing finds its appropriate image.

At such moments, the world-on-the-page seems to collapse into the 'outside' world where 'language always comes from some place',[14] where battles for space are always going on, even on the margins ('Women are ...'), especially on the margins. This is perhaps clearest with success stories. Representing the outsider is, after all, a thoroughly acceptable thing to do, witness (for example) Françoise Sagan's career. As love affairs with literature go, hers was a dream of consummation – fame at eighteen with her first novel, *Bonjour Tristesse* (1954); and then a long post-lude to the happy ending:

> I became a commodity, a thing, the Sagan myth. . . . I was ashamed of myself. . . . I was being trapped into a role and I couldn't get out of it. A life sentence of going to bed with sordid drunken characters . . .[15]

The particular irony of this is of course that the role she'd chosen was that of the Bohemian, the free spirit:

> I love those fleeting moments when people have had a few drinks and begin to be a bit unsteady. They let themselves go, stop acting and take their clothes off. They take off their masks and begin to say something real.[16]

Sagan looking back (these quotations come from *Réponses* in 1974, an 'imaginary interview' with herself, based on actual interviews she gave over twenty years) sees her writing life as a long struggle with what she was seen *as*, a struggle 'with', not exactly 'against'.

At its inception, and in its reception, writing joins itself onto the body of preconceived, possible books ('I raise my eyes to the books . . .'), which is perhaps what makes the notion of androgyny tempting. The history of that image of the 'creative marriage', though, from Plato on, is hardly encouraging: the theory says that the dissolution and merging of gender identity is what creation (on the model of procreation) is all about, but of course the theory's actually based on homosexual love, so that the 'breeding' involved is properly metaphorical, and no sex difference is in question. Elizabeth Smart's *By Grand Central Station* points up the paradoxes, when the lover/male muse reverts to type leaving her heroine with 'the insane loneliness of the first split amoeba':[17] he has a tomorrow, 'Tomorrow', indeed, personified as 'an ardent boy of Socrates' with whom he will inhabit the visionary upper world where creation is a magical game, whereas she – pregnant in truth – is exiled from artifice, since birth, bringing forth, and so on, the labour of love, are no longer visionary metaphors. One recalls that Aristophanes' fable in *The Symposium* makes heterosexual 'wholes' into the third sex. His originally spherical humans (male, female and hermaphrodite) split down the middle by the gods for cart-wheeling too blissfully and being sufficient unto themselves are *all* now mere splinters doomed to seek their essential other halves, but it is clear that same-sex seekers start with more clues.

When lovers meet, says Aristophanes, they clasp each other so desperately because each wants 'intimately to mix and melt and to be melted together with his beloved, so that one should be made out of two.'[18] I quote from Shelley's translation of *The Symposium* because Shelley (perhaps this is why Stead 'loved' him) was much concerned with the notion of the (creative) marriage, as the site of, and precondition for, what he platonically called creative 'thought' and writing. He allegorised his actual marriages: the first, to Harriet, turned the two-into-one idea into cruel travesty. To begin with he galvanised Harriet into a dazzle with idealist electricity. Later he accused her of having been creatively null, a corpse: 'a dead and living body had been linked together in loathsome and horrible communion.'[19] He felt himself diminished by contagion, 'sunk into a premature old age of exhaustion, which renders me dead to everything'.[20] He is echoing the Milton of the divorce tracts, another vengeful victim of the search for the poet's 'other half', though in Shelley's case disenchantment followed from meeting another woman (Mary Wollstonecraft Godwin; her very name implied she'd know about such things) who revealed Harriet for the loving sham she was, mirroring back his opinions so obligingly that she returned him to his loneliness. In Mary he found himself convincingly redoubled. ('In our family,' her 'sister' Claire Clairmont wrote, 'if you cannot write an epic poem or novel that by its originality knocks all other novels on the head, you are a despicable creature, not worth acknowledging.')[21] 'To mix and melt and to be melted together ...' Creative love is recognition, like to like. Mary Shelley's inspired comment on this was *Frankenstein*. She must, of course, as the poet's other half, write ('He was forever inciting me to obtain literary reputation'),[22] but what she produced was a classic fantasy of otherness and rejection. 'My hideous progeny',[23] as she calls it with maternal pride, depicts not only the injustice with which a creator corrupts his creature, but also (picking up the inevitable metaphor) a man who feels himself tied to a walking corpse, which happens – as has often been pointed out – to be more human, more rational and more imaginatively versatile than himself.

This brief digression on androgyny helps explain, I think, why women's love affair with literature has so often produced a 'Gothic' distribution of space, both within particular works and (in the case of 'displaced' writers like Stead, Rhys, Smart) in terms of reception and the canon. (Rosamund Lehmann, another rediscovered writer, has talked of feeling 'post-humous'.) Feminist criticism of the last decades has, in a sense, reinvented Aristophanes' jokey implication that heterosexual 'wholes' are somehow anomalous, monstrous. Penelope Shuttle and Peter Redgrove, for instance, speaking the language of two-in-one, sound more like candidates for a three-legged race:

> By and large, we do not think of each other as that man or that woman; we think of each other as Peter and Penelope; and in writing each is simultaneously the other's Sibyl and Scribe. We are trying to suggest that men and women learn from each other, but, because woman has been feared and betrayed, there is a balance due, and this has to be redressed by work on the man's part.[24]

True, Redgrove and Shuttle (like the Shelleys) are a specially literal instance of the notion of the text as a sexual meeting-place. The writers I've mentioned are, perhaps, special too in the degree of disproportion they suggest between the 'space' the world of letters seems to offer, and its simultaneous unfreedom. None the less, I'd argue that they merely show the wider situation writ large. A major effect of feminist criticism has been to redistribute textual space, and to stress how ubiquitous and difficult the paradoxes of writing's 'autonomy' are. In the process, the world on the page (the heterocosm?) has revealed its fissures and false promises, its closets and attics, its separate traditions. Writing as a labour of love (which I take to be one of the sub-texts of Stead's title, *For Love Alone*) has become ironised in the one ('androgynous') direction, privileged in others, through from 'Gothic' to separate communities of women, and the various, more or less radical versions of writing as equivo-cation, on the edge of silence – diaries, autobiography, strategies for writing between the lines.

Our sense of the available space is changing. Indeed, many

contemporary women writers are producing more or less metaphorical 'space-fictions' about finding more room. Christina
Stead, working through her heroine's options with her usual
thoroughness, gave her, at the very latest moment, a glimpse of
a future landscape:

> at present she had merely fought through that bristling black and
> sterile plain of misery ... beyond was the real world, red, gold,
> green, white, in which the youth of the world would be passed; it
> was from the womb of time she was fighting her way and the first
> day lay before her ... there was something on the citied plain for all
> of them, the thousands like thin famished fire.[25]

This moment of clairvoyance undoes any prospect of a happy
ending. Stead's Teresa, it is implied, has mutated or meta-
morphosed into a native utopian. Or to put it another way, she
has graduated from the love school she once dreamed about, not
by renouncing her mythomania but by trusting it: her 'real'
world is one that waits to be invented. Stead's plot presents
Teresa with the 'right' man only, it seems, to emphasise her
restlessness, her nostalgia for the future. Something of the same
happens in Doris Lessing's *The Marriages between Zones Three,
Four, and Five*, where separate, imagined cultures based on
gender differences – Zone Three a magical matriarchy, Zone
Four aggressively male, Zone Five a realm of nomads with an
Amazon queen – clash and 'marry'. Here, too, the effect is to set
off a process of restless change and mutual invasion. The
'natural' sex roles are seen quizzically, in a comic middle
distance:

> 'You, like red then?'
> 'I think I like you,' said he, in spite of himself grabbing at her – for
> he did not, he liked her even less than before ... he had in fact
> forgotten the independence of her, which informed every smile,
> look, gesture.
> She evaded him and slid away into the room, with a mocking
> backward look over her shoulder which quite astounded her – she
> did not know she had it in her![26]

This 'he' and 'she' do contrive to love one another, but the effect
is not to synthesise their separate realms, being taken out of

themselves sends them off in different directions, to new 'Zones'. She finds herself on the (unmarked) frontier of Zone Two, a place not envisaged in the title, where there are no marriages, and (possibly) no bodies, a place where 'she was at home, even while she recognised nothing at all'.[27]

The Marriages Between Zones Three, Four, and Five is (to date at least) untypical of the *Canopus in Argos* series it belongs to in making sexual love its catalyst for 'a re-making and an inspiration'. The other four take on the question of who appropriates language, why and how fictional space is mapped out, in a more abstract way. Sexual politics becomes, in these books, an aspect of politics, and political rhetoric of all sorts is seen as a misunderstanding of the nature of differing and difference. Lessing, of course, ever since *The Golden Notebook* was read as being 'about the sex-war', has insisted in many ways and in various tones of voice that books are indeed 'anybody's'. The *Canopus* series is, among other things, an attempt to find a 'new' space, a no man's land where both gender and genre are merely provisional. It is a project that is less utopian than a topian – and it points up the paradoxes of literary space.

Lessing and Atopia

> Nothing they handle or see has substance, and so they repose in their imaginations on chaos, making strength from the possibilities of a creative destruction. They are weaned from everything but the knowledge that the universe is a roaring engine of creativity, and that they are only temporary manifestations of it.
>
> (Doris Lessing, *Re: Colonised Planet 5, Shikasta*, 1979)

Canopus in Argos circles back on Lessing's *Children of Violence* series, most particularly in its engagement with questions of ideological violence, and fiction's aspiration to transcend the war of words, or at the least, to postpone that war indefinitely. 'Atopia' is a notion borrowed from Barthes, who uses it to locate the text, or suspend it, in the world of language, and it is a useful starting-point because it brings into play spatial metaphors:

we are all caught up in the truth of languages, that is, in their regionality .... For each jargon (each fiction) fights for hegemony ... if power is on its side, it spreads everywhere ... but even out of power, even when power is against it, the rivalry is reborn, the jargons split and struggle among themselves, a ruthless *topic* rules the life of language; language always comes from some place, it is a warrior *topos*.[28]

Only the text is atopic, plural, paradoxically at peace. Is *Canopus* a text in this sense? Certainly, there is a striking coincidence between the atmosphere in which Lessing's fiction replays her early colonial themes and Barthes's evocation of the curious calm that prevails in the modern text, as, for example, Betsey Draine[29] has pointed out. The regionality of language, its coming 'always from some place', and the way in which the languages of opposition 'split and struggle among themselves' – these were the peculiar agonies of *Children of Violence*. Early on, in *Martha Quest*, for example, we're told that, 'each group, community, clan, colour, strove and fought away from each other in a sickness of dissolution ... as if the principle of separateness was bred from the very soil.'[30] These are, too, recognisably enough, among the problems the *Canopus* series space-shuttles into no man's land.

The space fiction seems to take on the guilty colonial drives towards expansion and development, and take the harm out of them. Lessing the writer has, as she says in the prefatory remarks to *Shikasta*, 'made – or found – a new world for myself, a realm where the petty fates of planets, let alone individuals, are only aspects of cosmic evolution expressed in the rivalries and inter-actions of great galactic empires'.[31] Her tone suggests that her 'new world' ('made – or found') is empty space for expanding into, but in the event it is something more problematic. Repetition, indeed, turns out to be one of its main formal and thematic conventions. Here I'm picking up on the 'colonising' metaphor, repeated from *Children of Violence*, which provides the framework for all the *Canopus* novels, with the exception of *Marriages* (and which is present perhaps even there). The persistent colonial model provides a focus for considering the newness of Lessing's new world and its possible pluralism. One odd indication that *Canopus* may not have proved plural enough: the recent-ish revelation that from around the time of the third novel, *The Sirian Experiments* in 1981, Lessing was planning and executing a special kind of literary hoax. She wrote and published the two novels that now appear as *The Diaries of Jane Somers* under the name of Jane Somers. Given her decentring of the narrative voice in *Canopus*, and her attacks on rhetoric that 'comes from some place', the invention of Jane Somers is suggestive in several ways. For the moment, I would like simply to recall that Lessing broke the sequence of *Children of Violence* around the third novel too, with *The Golden Notebook*. 'Jane Somers', it seems already safe to say, will not count anything like so much; but there is a hint here of a pattern, a need to break out of one's project, which, again, suggests that the new world has something (something problematic) in common with the old.

'Shedding the Rhetoric of Empire, which they are prepared to analyse with acumen and to reject with scorn and contempt, they become prisoners of the Rhetoric of oppositional groups.'[32] This is the weary voice of Canopus in *The Sentimental Agents in the Volyen Empire*, describing how yet another generation is conned and conscripted by the armies of words. Lessing's impatience to arrive at the end of what is called in *Shikasta* 'The Age of Ideology' is explicit, written out, announced. It is there too in the formal insistence that 'history' is a function of geography or cosmography, and in the 'archival' strategies that cut up and juxtapose the narratives. Talk of, say, 'the force of history', all the rhetoric of opposition, is bred from the soil in the form of people's atavistic need to belong to the group, to herd together. In *The Sentimental Agents* Canopus pays ironic homage to the urgency of this need by listing the proliferating names we (they?) have for designating difference: 'races, kinds, types, nations, classes, sorts, genders, breeds, strains, tribes, clans, sects, castes, varieties, grades, even species'.[33] From the Canopean point of view, difference is, as it were, what all these have in common. Their more fully evolved version of the group mind envisages a whole where differences co-exist, and Need with a capital N is studied and understood. And so on. This whole-versus-group theme shapes all the *Canopus* novels, and can be seen at work, for instance, in the large-scale irony of *The Sirian Experiments*, where the managerial narrator, Ambien, becomes a 'traitor' because she realises that all along the seemingly rival

Empire had included her. Or again, in *The Marriages between Zones Three, Four, and Five*, when the Zone Four women form themselves into what looks very like a women's movement, and get imaginatively lost as a result, on an untimely pilgrimage to Zone Three. The group turns out to be a travesty of the whole.

These plots both celebrate heterogeneity, and render it permanently provisional. My earlier quotation from *The Sentimental Agents* listing 'races, kinds, types, nations' etc. ends with the words 'all of them united by *waiting*'. So difference is, seemingly, depoliticised. Canopeans do not deal in debate; they are unable to explain themselves, and pursue a gnostic, paradoxical 'silent' speech that is meant to undermine rhetoric, and make others wait. A quotation from Ambien in *The Sirian Experiments*, describing a Canopean agent on a cultural mission to a primitive people:

> He spoke of places 'beyond the waters' where an advanced medicine was used based on local balances and earth forces .... They did *not* hear. They *could* not hear. I have never before seen so clearly and simply illustrated that law of development that makes a certain stage of growth impossible to an individual, a people, a planet: first they have to hear.[34]

In context this is crushingly ironic, since it is Ambien herself who is (still) primitive, and who is hard of hearing. Communication between different cultures is delayed, difficult, partial, never complete. Because (to use Barthes again): 'A ruthless topic *rules* the life of language; language always comes from some place.' Speaking is superseded by listening, waiting, 'reading'. Dialogue (like Platonic dialogue, like – presumably – Sufi teaching techniques) is about 'turning the mind round' so that you see new dimensions, new spaces, in what you already know. In *The Making of the Representative for Planet 8*, the Planet 8 people are supplied with microscopes for this purpose, so that they can see themselves as composite, a conglomerate of groups, mostly space.

Unsurprisingly, then, one of the most characteristic structuring devices is a kind of synecdoche. The quotation from Ambien, for instance, spells it out, in expansionist form: 'an individual, a people, a planet'. Whatever you name, in this grammar, is a version of the part-for-the-whole, or the other way about. Some more examples: 'Yet most societies, cultures – empires – can be described by an underlying fact or truth, and this is nearly always physical, geographical'; 'Our Empire isn't random, or made by the decisions of self-seeking rulers or by the unplanned developments of our technologies ... Our growth, our existence, what we are is a unit, a unity, a whole.'[35] This last example, which comes from a Canopean agent, more or less betrays the device by naming it: it is a device for pointing always towards an (unachieved) totality. Hence its ironising effect in relation to partial, party politics – 'Nearly all political people were incapable of thinking in terms of interaction, of cross-influences, of the various sects and "parties" forming *together* a whole, wholes.'[36] Lessing's Canopeans are guardians of difference (they immerse themselves in local conditions, incarnate themselves as historical individuals) and at the same time subverters of the politics of difference.

They are also, she has insisted, mere strategies themselves:

> The reason, we all know, why readers yearn to 'believe' cosmologies and tidy systems of thought is that we live in dreadful and marvellous times where the certainties of yesterday dissolve as we live. But I don't want to be judged as adding to a confusion of embattled certainties.[37]

This takes one back to the atopia of the text ('writers', she goes on to remind us, '"make things up", that is our trade'). She is, though, being disingenuous. It is not so much a question of whether readers 'believe in', say, reincarnation, or angelic visitors, but of how the narrative voice represents the reader, how the text lets its readers in, and what it lets them in for. *Canopus* is all about the way different cultures occupy ultimately the same space; built into the texture is the assumption that one language, one group-code is always part of another larger one. Lessing has of course been talking about this throughout her writing life, and seems to have become conscious of it because she was a communist and a colonial – that is, a member of an oppositional minority within a dominant minority, neither of which acknowledged the positive meaning of race or gender. As I have argued elsewhere, her sense of herself as writer is shaped by the conviction that writing is about *being representative* (not necessarily representational).[38]

Two quotations, far apart in time. First, from her 1957 essay 'The Small Personal Voice':

> one is a writer at all because one represents, makes articulate, is continuously and invisibly fed by, numbers of people who are inarticulate, to whom one belongs, to whom one is responsible.[39]

And second, from the Preface to *The Sirian Experiments* in 1981:

> with billions and billions and billions of us on this planet, we are still prepared to believe that each of us is unique, or that if all the others are mere dots in a swarm, then at least *I* am this self-determined thing, my mind my own. Very odd this.... How do we get this notion of ourselves?
>
> It seems to me that ideas must flow through humanity like tides.[40]

The tone has changed a lot, of course, but the underlying need to locate an authorial 'I' that is potentially 'we' is still there. That she has invented a space-fiction format in pursuit of it is a measure, it seems to me, of the intensity of her built-in dread of the regional, the partial – 'white' Africa, in short.

The most striking legacy, in *Canopus*, is the structuring assumption that different groups inevitably overlap and interfere with each other, so that – to put it crudely – it is not a matter of oppression *or* co-existence, but of 'good' colonisers or 'bad' colonisers. The Canopeans (the good) are the group of groups, always at work to turn wars of words into silent symbiosis, and so on, agents of a (mostly) invisible Empire. And they are – despite their modest disguises – figures of authority, unmistakeably. Residual authority, perhaps, but all the more absolute for that. Consider this exchange from *The Making of the Representative for Planet 8*:

> 'Again, one person, one individual is made to represent so many!' And, as I spoke, I felt now familiar pressures, the announcement deep in myself of something I should be understanding.
>
> And that was when I let myself go away into sleep, having taken in what I could for that time. And when I woke, Johor was sitting patiently, waiting for me to resume. I had not done much more than register: Here I am! – and add to it the thought: But the 'I' of

me is not my own, cannot be, must be a general and shared consciousness – when Johor said . . .[41]

This specimen of 'dialogue' (one of many similar, repeated 'exchanges') demonstrates the power of silence. Johor, spokesman of Canopus, uses silence to undercut Doeg's speech, and prompt him to a 'recognition', a kind of invented memory of 'shared consciousness'. It demonstrates too the much greater authority of something you seem to arrive at yourself, compared with anything you are told. In short, Canopean silence is an insidious style of anti-rhetorical rhetoric, more potent than speech because it seems to come from everywhere and nowhere, from within, from the landscapes glimpsed in dreams . . . And so Planet 8 is colonised or, in Canopus-speak, evolves into a multiple monad, a voice that says 'we'. And 'we', fairly clearly here, is an imperial, imperative pronoun, 'something I *should* be understanding'.

Lessing's Canopeans employ a double-speak that appropriates the voices of others. This is less a way of renouncing authorial power, than of retaining it, by identifying with difference. Their patience and their ubiquity make them, in fact, remarkably pure figures of power, the latest (perhaps the last) inheritors of the tradition *Children of Violence* battled with, according to which (in Nicole Ward Jouve's words, my own are wearing thin) 'the world of an individual could be put into correspondence with, *represent*, the world'.[42] Lessing, who made her own way into the territory of the *nouveau roman* in *The Golden Notebook*, is now exposing equally unerringly, autodidact-fashion, the contradictions that lurk in the space of the *text*. Her scornful rejection of the 'Rhetoric of oppositional groups' serves to uncover once again 'the Rhetoric of Empire', transposed. Foucault, on the way the author has refused to die provides a striking analogy:

> In current usage . . . the notion of writing seems to transpose the empirical characteristics of the author into a transcendental anonymity . . . it keeps alive, in the grey light of neutralisation, the interplay of those representations that formed a particular image of the author. . . . There seems to be an important dividing line between those who believe that they can still locate today's discontinuities in the historico-transcendental tradition of the nineteenth

century, and those who try to free themselves once and for all from that tradition.[43]

Lessing's *Canopus* series criss-crosses this dividing line.

My argument has been that Lessing's excursion into space has exposed how thoroughly her language 'comes from some place'. In distancing her narrative voice from the 'warring certainties' of what she would see as *local* politics, she has arrived at a bleak picture of cultural imperialism. The celebrations of difference in *Canopus* are undercut and contradicted by a totalising urge, which becomes more (not less) insistent by virtue of the postponement of total order. And this, I think, is what is most interesting about her space-fiction; though it seems paradoxical to say so, because it is also what accounts for the large tracts of greyness and the sensation of *déjà vu*. One is tempted to locate these books in atopia because their combination of continuous local uncertainty and bland authority is anomalous and embarrassing. But they are more provocative and alive as anomalies. They remind us that dialogue is seldom conducted between equals, and that the writer in certain crucial senses 'speaks for' and represents the reader. The reader – this reader at any rate – often feels dismissed, excluded. Or, since I'm using the term 'colonised', by a benevolent (and therefore even more exasperating) authority.

Her new world is *not* different, in this sense, not *different* at all. Heterogeneous elements are not for her contiguous, or merely co-existent, but always rearranging themselves into parts and wholes. Thinking back to her African Stories, and to *Children of Violence*, one can detect the persistence of a thoroughly political, if unmanageable perception: that the adventure of discovery is always a matter of moving into space *already* inhabited by other kinds, other species, other codes. Which in its turn means that power struggles are not transcended, but transposed. Lessing has not emigrated to atopia. Witness 'Jane Somers', a mundane, woman's voice invented out of the strain (surely) of maintaining the long wait, the interminable delay of *Canopus*. The Jane Somers books are 'boulder-pushing' novels in the spirit of the end of *The Golden Notebook*: novels about personal responsibility in particular relationships. They are also (to keep the contradictions alive) another manifestation of Lessing's desire to disperse her authorial authority - as if it wasn't dispersed enough. As, I have argued, it isn't - *Canopus* is about claustrophobia in space. The problem of decentring the author seems for Lessing so far insoluble (though the Somers hoax was a witty comment on it). Or to put it another way: the world of words is still a battleground, and it is precisely the kind of nostalgia for the future these novels reveal which makes us know it, for better and for worse.

Notes

1. Christina Stead, *Sydney National Times*, 29 March/4 April 1981, p. 34.
2. Christina Stead, *For Love Alone* (Virago, London, 1978), p. 76.
3. Ibid.
4. Jean Rhys, *Smile Please* (André Deutsch, London, 1979), p. 62.
5. Elizabeth Smart, *By Grand Central Station I Sat Down and Wept* (Polytantric Press, London, 1977), pp. 46-7.
6. Ibid., p. 101.
7. Christina Stead, *For Love Alone* p. 122.
8. Desmond Hawkins, *The Listener*, 1 November 1945, p. 502.
9. Elizabeth Smart, *The Assumption of the Rogues and Rascals* (Granada, London 1978), p. 75.
10. Ibid., p. 109.
11. Ibid., p. 83.
12. Jean Rhys, *Sleep it off Lady* (Penguin, Harmondsworth, London, 1979), p. 127.
13. Jean Rhys, *Tigers are Better Looking* (Popular Library, New York, 1976).
14. Roland Barthes, *The Pleasure of the Text*, trans. Richard Miller (Farrar, Straus & Giroux, New York, 1975), p. 28.
15. Françoise Sagan, *Réponses*, trans. David Macey (Ram Publishing Co., Godalming, England, 1980), p. 40.
16. Ibid., p. 141.
17. Elizabeth Smart, *By Grand Central Station*, p. 122.
18. P. B. Shelley, *Prose Works*, ed. H. B. Forman (London, 1880), Vol. III, p. 191.
19. P. B. Shelley, *Letters*, ed. Frederick L. Jones (Clarendon University Press, Oxford, 1964), Vol. I, p. 383.
20. Ibid., p. 264.
21. *The Life and Letters of Mary Wollstonecraft Shelley* (London 1889), Vol. II, p. 248.
22. Mary Shelley, *Frankenstein* (London 1888), p. vi.
23. Ibid., p. xi.

24. Penelope Shuttle and Peter Redgrove, 'The Dialogue of Gender', *On Gender and Writing*, ed. Michelene Wandor (Pandora Press, London 1983), p. 144.
25. Christina Stead, *For Love Alone*, p.494.
26. Doris Lessing, *The Marriages Between Zones Three, Four and Five* (Jonathan Cape, London 1980), p. 66.
27. Ibid., p. 193.
28. Roland Barthes, *The Pleasure of the Text*, p. 28.
29. Betsey Draine, *Substance Under Pressure* (University of Wisconsin Press, 1983), p. 28.
30. Doris Lessing, *Martha Quest* (1952) (Panther, St Albans 1966), p. 56.
31. Doris Lessing, *Shikasta* (1979) (Panther, St Albans, 1981), p. 8.
32. Doris Lessing, *The Sentimental Agents in the Volyen Empire* (Jonathan Cape, London 1983), p. 79.
33. Ibid., p. 161.
34. Doris Lessing, *The Sirian Experiments* (1981) (Panther, St Albans, 1982), p. 263.
35. Ibid., p. 80; *The Making of the Representative for Planet 8* (1982) (Panther, St Albans, 1983), p. 80.
36. Doris Lessing, *Shikasta*, p. 101.
37. Doris Lessing, *The Sirian Experiments* p. 10.
38. Lorna Sage, *Doris Lessing* (Methuen, London and New York, 1983), p. 46.
39. 'The Small Personal Voice', in Paul Schlueter (ed.), *A Small Personal Voice* (Vintage Books, New York, 1975), pp. 20-1.
40. Doris Lessing, *The Sirian Experiments*, p. 11.
41. Doris Lessing, *The Making of the Representative for Planet 8*, p. 89.
42. Nicole Ward Jouve, 'Of Mud and Other Matter: *The Children of Violence*', in Jenny Taylor (ed.), *Notebooks / Memoirs / Archives: Reading and Rereading Doris Lessing* (Routledge & Kegan Paul, London, 1982), pp. 75-134, 126.
43. Michel Foucault, 'What is an Author?', in J. V. Harari (ed.), *Textual Strategies* (Methuen, London, 1979), pp. 141-60, 144-5.

2

'HER LEGS BESTRID THE CHANNEL': WRITING IN TWO LANGUAGES

Nicole Ward Jouve

> His legs bestrid the Oceans; his reared arm
> Crested the world . . .
> > *(Anthony and Cleopatra)*
>
> They give birth astride a grave
> > (Beckett, *Waiting for Godot*)

I live and write in two languages: French and English. No great shakes to be striding such a divide: thousands do it; many women feel themselves caught between three, four, five, languages; between a local and a national language. Many have swum the Channel. My arm isn't reared and if it were, all it could crest is my own head. Sorry, Cleopatra.

Yet it's not because a predicament lacks grandeur and originality that it isn't interesting. For doing the splits geographically, linguistically, poses problems of identity. It's a more graphic form of what women who strive to speak with their own voice experience anyway. Indeed, it's precisely because the situation is so wide-spread, because *mobility*, in terms of place, culture, speech, imaginary projection of self, affects more and more women, that it might be useful to try and work out what my own 'bilingualism' entails.

(And while I'm clearing my throat let me cough up a bit of phlegm.

34

I labour at, am in labour over, two languages. Yes, there is a divide, there is a gap between the two and I'm not that keen on bridges (more on subterranean tunnels?). But whatever else, the divide isn't death, isn't negation. Let me send the Godot-trapped pair, Didi and Gogo, back to back in their womanless hell. We do not give birth 'astride a grave'. The Channel, a pretty polluted and busy sea but a sea all the same, ebbs and flows between my two 'countries'. The grey-breasted robin that keeps perching over a slender bamboo stake above some yellow wallflowers, tipping its pretty head and swallowing the odd fly as it goes by, cares nothing for death. The man who gave me a book about bird-watching was buried yesterday. This morning, looking at the robin, what I want to do is mother the man quietly on into ongoing life, rejoicing at what he would have rejoiced at.

Bilingual Beckett, you cast a long shadow. I've been in it. Now I'm out.)

*   *   *

'Moitié-de-Poulet' goes on some errands

I am French – still. I have retained my French 'nationality'. Was born and bred in Marseilles and Provence, finished my 'studies' in Paris. I married a half-Irish 'Englishman' over twenty years ago, and with the exception of one year in Paris have been living in England (and English-speaking Canada) ever since. I have three 'English' children: bilingual, complex, with a wanderer's instinct about them and a taste for the cosmopolitan: but British. Going on like this makes me feel like a concentrate of the Smith family in Ionesco's *Bald Prima Donna*, where Mrs Smith announces that they drink English beer and eat English soup. A French journalist from *Elle* obviously saw me as such, writing, 'she wears English trousers and extraordinary laced-up English shoes' (beautiful antiques, seven quid in a jumble sale, and I was so proud of my find!). Ah well. To return: I recently calculated that exactly half of my life had now been spent in France, half in England. At this stage of equilibrium, I am a perfect mongrel.

There is a (French?) fairy-tale about a creature called 'moitié-de-poulet', 'half-chicken'. The illustrations show it as cut down the middle lengthwise, from head to tail. Moitié-de-poulet hops busily on its one paw and runs critical errands for the king. That's me. My French moitié-de-poulet perches on walls and meditates at windows, flapping its one rather ineffectual wing and on occasions using it as a parachute to glide down from the branch where it has imaginatively managed to perch. My English half-chicken pecks and pokes, generally looking for grub.

'Moitié-de-poulet' is about right. Half is half. My presence in one country, one language always means my absence from the other.

I had no childhood, no youth in England. Have none of the instinctive knowledge, the intimate relation to – green and water and 'long summer days' and the Battle of Britain and Monday wash and Thursday baking and 'Grammar' versus 'Comprehensive' and miners' cottages and terraced streets and pop music and India – which growing up in England in the 1940s and 1950s and early 1960s would have given me. I can hear class and region in accents, I can't reproduce it. I can in French, though. My English voice is the most peculiar mix of a foreigner's frozen state of development, short of the right intonations and rhythms, with an eerie pliancy, a large vocabulary. A freak. But a twenty-year-old freak. Old enough to vote (which I don't).

Conversely, I have no adulthood in France (or had virtually none till I started publishing with the Editions des femmes). May '68 I experienced through the English media and the reports of French friends. I know how crucial it was in the making of the consciousness of my generation and the generation immediately following it. I know that the disillusionment that followed was lethal for some. It wasn't so for me. I take 'dips' into the French political – I was going to say 'arena', but then my 'dips' would be sand-baths – here you are, you see: I am fumbling around for an 'English' equivalent for a nascent French metaphor: 'j'y ai trempé; je n'y ai pas été immergée: look at the mud I'm churning up! Well, I have not been immersed in May '68. The same applies to everything that's been happening to France in the last twenty years or so from Pompidou to Simone Veil and the resurgence of racism and the expansion of 'ordinateurs' and 'vacances de neige' to the odd

36

and multifarious ways in which streets change while remaining the same and idioms and coinages and slangs mutate from one year to another. When I go back, which is fairly frequently, I do notice bits and pieces, in the papers I read, the speech of my friends and of my friends' children. What do I do about it? Learn the new idioms 'by heart'? To 'modernise' my French? How odd, to be learning one's own language as if it were a foreign language. Or do I choose to speak and write a more and more antiquated French, quaint, like the silk of one's first ball-dress, kept in moth-balls in a carton or some out-of-reach drawer – without even the comfort of thinking that it'll come back into fashion (for language unlike fashion has no recurring cycles)? Is my 'native' language, through lack of air and moisture, becoming threadbare, its fibres, paper-thin? Will the day come when I can no longer write in it, when it will tear, flimsily shred like ancient silk?

No wonder I am obsessed with Miss Havisham.

Alas! it is not as if I had made all that good a use of English during these my adult years. For I have in some ways only half lived in England. Sometimes when it was cold and muddy, or even when August was lush, its light somehow tinged with black, I've been pining for the dryness, the cleanness of the smells, the bare rocks of my mediterranean south. Sometimes feeling the place, my Yorkshire place, was *unreal* (which is a weird and worrying feeling), the people – dare I say it – not quite 'human' 'English' detachment brings out of me, perversely, my most aloof and unavailable self – what my husband rightly rails at as my 'holier-than-thou' moods – a cataleptic stiffness of which I only become aware when something makes it break down. I was recently visited out of the blue, by an Irish mother-of-two who was unselfconsciously friendly, offered me her free train voucher, and went away warmly shaking my hand, having talked about *herself*. As she closed the door I was trembling with pleasure, and caught myself thinking, 'How good it is for a change to talk to a human being', which then made me blush because of all it implied. But then, there you are. Better own up. It's not a question of being French or English. It's a question of not being on the same wavelength. I'm sure English women who've, for instance, lived in Paris will have had similar experiences.

Politically too, it's very difficult to 'be' anywhere. Living so long in England and reading the English press, etc. makes you feel sympathetic to British positions, but at the same time you don't stop being sympathetic to French ones. So that whenever the two countries clash, which they frequently do, I find myself defending whichever one I'm not in to the people of the 'other side' – with predictable unpopularity. I make myself think of my mother, complaining that whenever she tried to 'explain' my brothers' 'position' to my father, he accused her of betraying him; whenever she tried to make my brothers see their father's 'point of view', they accused her of being biased. The fact is, you're not on *either* side. They're just not you. I can't, for instance, get reconciled with the anti-Europeanism of the British Left: how could *I* be anti-European? I dislike the lack of excitement about 'intellectual' matters, in this country, the suspicion about theory, about ideas. I find the way in which everything remotely connected with the 'avant-garde' (e.g. a few years back, structuralism) gets classed as 'left-wing' (even when it's somebody as right-wing as Lévi-Strauss) quite bewildering. On the other hand, I've been so distanced from 'theory', through lack of intellectual support and through the sheer 'materiality' of my life, that I now find some of the 'French' intoxication with, for instance, the language of psychoanalytic concepts nearly comic. Well, not quite. I find it strange, but I'm also peeved that I'm not more familiar with it. I certainly am more startled by it than I would be if I'd stayed in a slowly evolving milieu. I can still remember my sheer delight when a friend said, about another woman she disliked, 'She's got a superego as big as the Ritz.' It said it all perfectly. But I would never have come to such a formula in a month of Sundays. (I would have had to wait for the 'semaine des quatre jeudis' for that to occur to me in French.)

Talking English, I felt for a long time very much like a parrot. I was so aware of my efforts to adapt to the world of academic learning by imitation of mannerisms and formulas. I even remember noting words down when listening to university or 'clever' talk (you then said things were 'complex' and 'ambiguous' and you were 'concerned'; the only word I can congratulate myself on having abominated from the start is the awful 'surely'). I wanted to be able to use the 'tools' myself, you see. It took the fool that I was years to realise that tools shape your hand – words shape your mouth, your mind – that they equip you for the production of bookcases when it's perhaps bird's nests you'd like to be making. But there is no knowing that until you've suffered from having your desire knocked out of you. I once wrote a book about Baudelaire: the best bit was when on a rainy day I suddenly let the pattern of rain-drops on the window-pane in front of me lead me to a reflection about how I came by metaphor. The publishers said, all in a chorus, 'It's all very pretty, this "personal" touch, but really, you know, not quite serious.' So I cut it out. You have to do a lot of unlearning before you get to the position when you start growing a tongue of your own. Let official voices now fill somebody else's lungs.

I am talking about criticism. Which is what I have always written in English, my second, or second-hand language. Conversely, all my 'creative' prose has been written in French. It just happened that way. I didn't think consciously about it until a few years ago, when I was asked at a women's meeting to talk precisely on this subject of bilingualism, and I was suddenly struck by how consistent the split had been. Moitié-de-poulet indeed.

I had always 'written' in secret, ever since I had been a child. This need for secrecy, for privacy no doubt was fostered, or enhanced, by the kindly oppressiveness of the adult world round about me. I grew up in a large family town house which had been built by my great-grandmother. It did have something of a matriarchal set-up, my grandmother, whose favourite I was (I slept in my grandparents' bedroom till I was ten), very much ruling the roost. In the end, my grandparents ended up living on the third floor; my parents, three brothers and I, on the second; my uncle, aunt and four cousins, on the first; sundry (often spinsterly) relatives on other floors, the 'maids' on the fifth floor. Several of the maids got pregnant and had babies. Yet when I expressed to my mother my decision when I was grown-up to have children but no husband, she told me this would be impossible. I spent a lot of time with the maids, a lot of time with my grandmother, learning from them both the 'feminine' arts of sewing, knitting, crochet, embroidery, etc. I went to a kindly but deeply 'processive' Catholic school; and was so penetrated by a conviction of the righteousness of the adult world, that I remember once telling my mother that it must be a great relief to be grown-up, because then you did not sin any more. She answered, much to my surprise, that adults sinned too. But I didn't believe her: I was touched by how kind she was trying to be to me.

Adults, at school and home and church, watched you like hawks. The other children did too. When I first started with periods (which the women in the family, who all knew about it, treated as a nice catastrophe), you used washable towels. Mine were soaking in the bidet when my eleven-year-old cousin peeped in, took a good look at the bloody water, asked me with a big grin on his face whether I had hurt myself – the rage and embarrassment and sense of *impotent* exposure. So guess what I did when I finally got my own bedroom, and my grandmother bought me a desk with a secret drawer? Sorry to be so archetypally banal, but yes, of course, I wrote poems and stories and kept a diary and hid my notebooks in the secret drawer with dire warnings to anyone nosy enough to pry. I've always had a soft spot for spells.

Writing, I could cease to be 'good'. Cease to produce the show I felt the much-loved grown-ups required of me. I could dare and dream and be passionate, and pretend to be taller and wiser than myself, and nobody to call my bluff. Later, when I found myself married, a teacher and a mother, in a strange place, under a lot of strain, wanting to be a good wife and a good mother and a good housewife and a good teacher and frequently making a mess of things, the writing started again. Of course, at least half of the pressure originated in me. It was my fault, I presume, if I had this oversize superego (which a little something, thank God, just stopped short of being as large as the Ritz). If I had had 'character', I would have rebelled, and fought head on, in childhood as in adulthood. Instead of which I resorted to the old way out: I started writing fiction in French.

But it wasn't just escapism; not just 'return' to a childhood habit, seeking refuge in my 'native' language as something that was free from the adult pressures English and the academic life had come to represent for me. I was also trying to deal with the present in what was beginning to look as 'my' language: nothing like exile to make you tearfully, *viscerally* patriotic. The cord has been stretched, it's tugging at you. When it was nicely coiled in a corner, you never realised it was even there. So in some ways French began to function for me as a language of 'origins'. As a 'maternal' language, in opposition to English which I must have cast in the role of a 'patriarchal', a 'symbolic', a law-giving language. I didn't at all realise what I was doing at the time. But this must be why *Shades of Grey*, which I began to write in the late 1960s, opens with a story about a young French mother. She's just had a baby daughter; she's in an English, a strongly regimented, 'hysterical' maternity ward. She feels herself being gradually estranged from her own body, her own baby, by the rules and etiquette of the hospital. The English everyone talks about her becomes the expression of this estrangement. It is like the outside, the bleak air into which she is being forcibly delivered. She clings to soft, 'babble-like', 'poetic' French reminiscences as a defence against this. Revealingly, those bits proved untranslatable and were left out of the English edition. So were the pieces of exploratory, associative, dream-like prose at the end of the volume, the attempt by the narrator to 'grow a tongue' of her own. I readily agreed with the publishers that the 'English reader', that mysterious entity, just wasn't keen on that sort of writing. I must have been unwilling to have all that ground gained in French translated into the 'other' language: unwilling to come out of the 'womb' (?) where I had gone for shelter.

So, my practice would in some respect fall in with Cixous's (and Kristéva's) notions of a 'maternal' language. One that is 'of the body', pre-Oedipal, plentiful. What Cixous talks about when she describes her mother's linguistic intercourse with her as a child, as *milk*. As nourishing. Like those juices which Clarice Lispector's 'orange' produced for her. Also, in so far as French, which for months at a time I neither heard nor spoke, was being driven inwards and downwards, perhaps it assumed something archaic that had not been there before. That repressed and ideally unbroken language/self came to balance the multiplying incomplete selves that my 'social' life was creating: I was a 'different' person in the Yorkshire countryside where I was living from the academic self I was when at work from from from. I was turning into Dostoyevsky's double, selves springing up from the pavement. French then played the role of a dark, 'unconscious' stabilising force secretly taking me along the road where some day, some 'truth' might be found.

But that was also far from being the whole story. For the 'creative' French I started writing when I found myself living in England was a continuation (in a new setting) of a French I had attempted to devise whilst *growing up* as a reaction to the adult world which surrounded me, and the French 'culture' I was being introduced to. It had never been 'natural'. I had always experienced it as reactive, as constructed. For that matter, I think that not just me, but a lot of children who write start with a kind of imitative rhetoric. The models are different for boys and girls, and it would be interesting to work out what the differences are; but in my experience the *imitative* pattern is similar; only very *small* children (perhaps later very rebellious children) draw or write those things we associate with im-promptu surrealist genius. When children are over eight, or nine, or ten, especially of course when they are on a good-book-reading diet, they aspire to that magic self which they implicitly know is both behind and ahead of them, with 'literary' means. The books, poems, tales told by the grown-ups, have made them glimpse it. They think they've got to tread those paths to get to it. So it was at least for me. I remember thinking I was going to write *real* books for children, because the grown-ups being grown-ups had forgotten what it was like to be a child, and I knew. Well, I never did. The mirage of projection, of desire, concealed from me what some other part of me knew was essential. And so, paradoxically, English rendered me the service of making my French more 'natural' (in the sense of less and less conscious and controllable, cut off from models and a context, with 'roots' ever further away from sight). French, which I might be starved of, which might be starved of social, of 'external' sustenance for months on end, which might so totally disappear that I even dreamt in English, continued its subter-ranean or submarine existence somehow, mutating, I realised when it surfaced, in symbiosis with what had been going on in my 'conscious' spoken English world – in fact, developing social and political dimensions which had been there more faintly earlier. God knows how all the 'translations' occurred. What was interesting was that the French became deep – that when it did me the favour of coming out, I felt it was welling up.

But – I seem to be losing sight of the point – it was also a reaction to the present. Work upon the present. Transformation of the present. It was also a resistance to, a complicated game played with, censorship, where French and English weren't necessarily in the roles the previous 'maternal/patriarchal' opposition might suggest.

The impulses are so contradictory, so mixed up with those issues of secrecy Adrienne Rich powerfully indites, I can only work them out one at the time. I do it because, whilst I feel I am guilty of many of the failures in courage she describes, being honest about it is my only way ('back'?) to 'truth'.

I always write in secret. Individualism: the 'bourgeois' luxury of 'inner life'. Some of it is the superstitious fear that the power to write will evaporate once writing has made contact with air, been read by others, or even talked about. In that sense, writing in a 'foreign' language is a defence, like mirror-writing when one is an adolescent: I was very good at it. The more distant my 'French' writing life is from my English life, the safer I feel. But some of this compulsive privacy also goes back to the period when I knew I could be naughty when I wrote – to the unavowed conviction that it is 'wicked' to write. The sources of the taboo are too numerous and too complicated to be gone into. But that it is *also* 'real', also 'external', was proved to me when I wasn't really expecting it, upon the French publication of *Shades of Grey*. I thought the book was quite tame, didn't think of it as likely to give offence. So much water had gone over the bridge. So I was surprised when I heard from a relation that, for instance, my uncle's family had almost come to blows over it. That they were shocked, indignant. There was one good reason why they could have been, I knew – and felt afterwards rather penitent about it. But they sermonised me about my bad taste, bad language, for talking about what 'we all know about but don't talk about'. There was a (discreet) buggery scene in one of the stories. Two months later, my uncle and aunt sent me as a consciously innocent (I'm sure of that) Christmas present (their usual gift): two popular French books. One was an historical novel about my native Provence, and it started with the violent rape of the heroine. The other was the fond memoirs of an old Provençal hunter and man of letters, and it started with his recalling how, as a child, he used to enjoy poking his finger into

43

the anus of a deer freshly killed by his father. And I really got going over why what was being regarded as so monstrously shocking when I wrote about it from the point of view of the 'victim', and 'realistically', was so inconspicuous as to be almost nice, nicely 'literary' and polite, anyway, when men(?) wrote about it. I felt very strongly (it's one instance among many) that the lid was being slammed. It made me realise that I had gone 'north', had gone to live in England *also for freedom*: because there, I thought (till my children started being worried about what I was likely to write about), I felt there was nobody I cared about who cared about what I wrote. I didn't belong, I was nobody, I was anonymous. Well, I think I was wrong: you can't escape. But perhaps if you moved all the time, changed countries and identity fast enough, you could keep that particular censoring dog at bay. I tried. I wrote *L'Entremise* as an attempt to operate within the suffocating field of censorship. On one level it paid: it's been the only non-critical work I have written which my family found likable. On another level it starved me, turned into a Doppelganger story ... and of course, the forbidden at the end made such a return that it deeply affected my mother, so strong was one moment of 'recognition' for her.

That whole period made me both 'see' the taboos, and take a despairing measure of my own inescapable tendency to give offence. Of course, in a way, everything is taboo: your family, your friends, all sexual matters, deep feelings. How come I can't write 'nice' books like so many people? Is it that I am particularly wicked, perverse? And so I have flirted with the possibility of anonymity – better than even a foreign language, the possibility to write *as far as you want*, and not to have to live with the consequences ... I nearly did, when I published my case study of the Yorkshire Ripper case. I felt that by putting my name on it, I was stepping even more clearly into the danger zone: 'he' can see you ... I was helped there – helped to a name, that is – by the fact of writing in French, of having French at work on the data, foreignness to give distance to the case. I also enjoyed the support of the Editions des femmes: the enterprise became plural. I wasn't alone. But the fact remains that there are things I have written, and many more I want to write, which I couldn't bear to own up to. So whether to keep them 'hidden' for ever, wait till I'm so old nothing matters anymore, or go for anonymity . . .

This is where a contradiction is at work. I also 'inherited' from long religious training a belief in 'writing as salvation', 'writing as truth'. That whole western tradition of transference of the religious to 'art' – that's got me too. So while on one level I feel writing = bad = secret, theft, treachery, I am also persuaded that writing = salvation = the truth at *any* cost, and somewhere, something in me means *any*. And there 'secret' means 'what will eventually come out', means 'sacred'. Pressure, taboos, mean the building-up of the necessary steam, something like revving up. Lies mean, not lies but creating the elaborate conditions within which 'truth' might be glimpsed.

And here another twist occurs. Recently, it happened that two pieces came out 'in English', and that they seemed to be driving deeper, into areas of the mystical, areas also of my infancy and my children's infancy, areas that I had come to suppose only French could get to, or back to. Part of the reason why this was so, I suppose, was that, feeling terrified by my sense of the peculiarity of my English, I was trying to descend somewhere where English, such as something in me can feel it, could make its own 'essential' noise. Sound like itself, in so far as my own bizarre linguistic gifts and inadequacies could allow it to sound at all. I went deep-water fishing, that is, but wonderfully it turned out that, as I didn't know where I was in relation to the water (whether above or inside, nor how many waters inside waters there were), it got me to feel I might write about things I hadn't dared touch upon in French. There was something impersonal about English that made a certain type of quest possible. French phrases, like old boots and rusty tin cans, came up at the end of my hook . . . Wouldn't it be lovely if that led me into that 'maternal' kingdom I thought English was denying . . . And if it did, in what language would that happen?

* * *

Translation and Schizophrenia

For many bilingual women, Jacqueline Risset most notably perhaps,[1] translation is an activity by means of which the 'natural' bond 'meaning-language' can be transgressed. It is a state of continued suspension – a living process, ever beginning anew, allowing, in Walter Benjamin's words, 'the post-maturation of the foreign speech, the birth throes of one's own speech'. The process, therefore, is eminently 'feminine'. When you translate, the absolute status of nouns, the 'Name-of-the-Father', is shaken. Exchanges between words are no longer 'full', that is, guaranteed by the law of the Father, the law of significance. Identities cease to be stable. You escape from definition, from the law which rules and partitions women, which prevents femininity from coming into being. Translation = no man's land = woman's land?

Whilst translating, black and white cease to be the rule: you positively move inside the spectrum of grey. But I discovered, somewhat to my cost, when I was translating *Le Spectre du Gris* into *Shades of Grey* that, instead of making me inhabit a transgressive or birth throes state, translation turned the spectrum of grey into the *spectre* of grey. The punning is not so flippant as it sounds; it has a long, a real, history. The activity of translating destroyed whatever bit of identity the writing of the stories had constructed for me in French. It threw me back into the horror of indifferentiation, of possible non-sense. I found that in order to translate, you have to have a non-questionable identity in one language. You simply can't afford to do it, if you're split, if you're two bizarrely osmotic 'moitiés-de-poulet'. Translating made me feel sick. What had happened was that, in some of the stories at least, I had already 'translated' mostly 'English' experiences into (a) fiction, (b) French, (c) layers of significance that had to do with those other translations. Moving into English was retrogressive, 'realistic' in the wrong sense of the word. I was unweaving what I had woven. I was destroying a painfully elaborated ... not identity, but a way of being that enabled you/me to be free from black and white, to move inside working contraries, inside a form that stopped things from being definite. The form did function in French, partly because certain contexts, allusions, were immediately perceptible, partly because the fiction/translation was being woven at first hand. Trying to put it all into English gave the fabric the wrong sort of status (too definite) as well as making it un-matchable and bizarrely vulnerable. Above all, I realised that my own mental sanity depended upon my operating as *two* people, two writers:

one French, the other English. That I did not like *moving* from the one to the other: in fact I do everything to perpetuate and feed the difference. I'm glad there *is* a Channel, that the sheer journeying from one place to the other is so burdensome. Every time I do that journey, I feel as if I'm going through mutations as strong as those that befall Alice when she eats cakes and nibbles at mushrooms. A similar thing happens when I have to translate 'for keeps' (the job of impromptu, fluid, run ;-of-the-mill interpreting, translating as you go poses no problems). Possibilities proliferate. The two languages become gaping chasms. The perspective of having to arrive at a finished, 'written' object that would posit a living and *perceptible* correlation between the two languages is somehow unbearable to me. The sense of being suspended in mid-air, the way the two languages start affecting each other, like spilt water-colours that run into each other, gradually makes me unable to know where either is. I become anguished about spelling; words, phrases, become odd; I no longer know whether you can 'say this', whether it is 'correct'. I realise then that I need the partition, the cut between the two. I am perhaps not so far away from schizophrenia as I'd like to think. I can live as two people. I'd go mad if the two people were forced to acknowledge each other, rather than go their separate ways, the way it pleases each.

The only solution I found about translating my own stuff (I try to avoid having to translate others) was to re-write. Make it into a different object. Let the grain of whatever language I'm moving in impose its pattern. If it's oak it's tight. I love the way English can rely upon prepositions, short words, imperative or telegraphic modes. By contrast, I have found that I often get on to something interesting, or simply get to wherever I feel that I must be, by doing, with French, what Philippe Sollers calls 'flocculation': abundant flowering, thick as the petals of a carnation, hovering like a hummingbird, whose multiple spiralling wing-beats maintain it in the air long enough for it to get at a flower. What is certain is that the decision to write in one language rather than another is going to lead to something different. I shall never end being amazed by how heterogeneous France and England are. Where would I be if I could do the same thing in both?

Drowned, of course: in the grey waters of the Channel.

*　　*　　*

Possession

Yet I am also in the business of connections.

Connections with what is, or seems to be, totally different from me.

Taking a character who is as unlike me as I can possibly imagine. The beautiful model of *L'Entremise*, its narcissistic heroine – and seeing 'ce qui reste quand on a tout enlevé'. What's left when you've removed every way to identification with, love for, a character. (Interesting what it did to George Eliot when she created Rosamund Vincy.)

Trying to create 'people' whom, on account of class, colour, a whole range of experience, I could never hope to know – who would neither wish to know me themselves, nor feel I had any right to get to know about them, write about them. And yet write about them, because somehow there *is* a bond between us and it is important to see what it is. But it is just as important not to take possession, not to 'give' people a 'voice'. Not to make them signify, be recuperable, exploitable. I get very moved by the way Virginia Woolf 'did' Septimus Warren Smith in *Mrs Dalloway*. You can feel she was 'trying', you can feel the strain, and there is nothing perhaps more lovable in the writers we love than where they haven't quite pulled it off, where the ropes show: their passing weakness suddenly touches our prevailing weakness; we feel the warmth of their 'humanity'. Virginia Woolf knew she had little in common with a 'lower-class' young man suffering from shell-shock: she'd never even *seen* the war. And yet she knew with a knowledge bought at the cost of madness that there was a link between Septimus Warren Smith and Mrs Dalloway, and she set about discovering it. Her hovering round that bond (the way Mrs Ramsay tries to make her dinner-party work) that *is* translation, of the kind Jacqueline Risset talks about.

I understood something of this when trying to end my analysis of the Yorkshire Ripper case. I wrote a piece of fiction, mostly in the second person, the 'tu' of one of the victims who came from Spain originally. I wanted to reaffirm the 'humanity' of those women whom everyone, the killer and the police and the judiciary and the media, had been almost systematically defacing. I called the piece 'An Elegy for a Dead Prostitute', and I tried to make it into a song, something 'open', as close to 'poetry' as I could get. I thought of Genet's 'transformations', of his covering his convicts with flowers. I used 'tu' because I knew I couldn't be her, I had no right to say 'I', or 'she', to pretend that I knew either way. But saying 'tu' is also a way of being fraternal – of making it happen to the reader as well. The 'bond' was that, however privileged I might be and underprivileged she had been, we were both 'immigrants' from the Mediterranean. No, that wasn't enough. But yes, it was enough: I wasn't trying 'realistically' to produce her voice: in any case, she would have spoken some sort of Spanish English, and I was writing in French: in fact, I could *hear* the top of her palate rubbing over some consonants. I was trying to create an area of language where a voice such as hers might be heard.

Still, about connections: what is odd is that you may work on, discover, something that seems totally private, even eccentric, in a state of total isolation – and it turns out to have an unexpectedly political, a public, face. Sometimes the discovery is pleasant. Many times I have dreamed of a book, cherished an idea, in the secret of my brain or chambers or wherever one thinks privacy is at its greatest, only to discover that I was plotting, or doing, exactly what large sections of the French 'intelligentsia' were up to. It nearly makes you believe in all sorts of suspect things: 'nationality' (somehow, something – what? – the 'formation' you've been given? the language? – makes you remain on a wavelength even though you're abroad, in another context altogether, and you don't know that you are); the famous *Zeitgeist*; or Doris Lessing's concentric circles, what she calls 'ripples from the storm': the same thoughts, 'fads', mysteriously carried by atmospheric mental waves, reach a wide range of apparently disconnected people. Whichever way it is, I have seen the phenomenon occur so often that I now take it for granted: if I have this wonderful 'original' idea, ten to one that a lot of other people are having it too. For instance, I worked on the case of the Yorkshire Ripper in total solitude and with a certain 'pioneering' feeling; I found on arriving in Paris when the book came out that the whole town was ablaze with interest in 'fait-divers': countless books were coming out, special issues of magazines, debates in the Pompidou Centre, even an exhibition in the Musée des Arts et Traditions Populaires. I nursed in secret for years plans for a picaresque erotic novel about a woman's multiple loves, only to find on my last visit that a large number of other French ladies had written exactly along those lines - not least among them Kristéva - and that Sollers had produced the male counterpart to my idea. But nothing like this is happening in England that I can see: it's all debates about 'pornography' or 'romance' ...

Also, sometimes one has the hallucinatory feeling that what's happening on a local, or private level is the *expression* of a larger public event. Thus my university department had its own incestuous mini-Watergate at the time of the American one. What was amazing was how the stages of its development seemed to be mimicking the other, how it all seemed to lay bare the same inner structures or political predicament as the 'real' one. Whether the mind is so thirsty for metaphor that it *projects* all this, or whether, like a major disease, a particular 'crisis' proliferates secondary ailments all over, I don't claim to know. One summer many years ago I became obsessed by the Fisher-Spassky chess confrontation. As day after day I read the papers about it, it looked as if its episodes corresponded to the vicissitudes of a relationship I was going through at the time. I nearly learnt to play chess on the strength of this! Thinking that perhaps, once I understood the *actual* moves of the game, I might get to the bottom of what was possessing me. The mood passed, Spassky (with whom I had identified, of course) lost, Fisher disappeared into the solitude of some New York hotel bedroom.

What is more worrying is to discover that you've been moved by something - again, something public - that you didn't know at the time was moving you. More pretentiously, let me say that the writing of fiction (which is supposedly 'private', imaginative) can turn out to be the expression of something much larger, more impersonal. It's all very well to say this is a pretty old 'sociology of lit.', or 'Marxist' idea: it's a different matter studying the thing and having it happen to you. For me, *L'Entremise* started with the tale of a woman who overhears her own voice in the *back* of the car she's driving, then sees her own 'double's' *aged* face appear in the rear mirror in the place of her

50

own *young* face. She then gets hounded by her 'double', who always creeps up to her stealthily, from behind. I had actually heard my own voice in the back of the car – and been frightened of what was at the back. Anyway, the book came out; and it was only two years later, when I had finished work on the Ripper case, that it occurred to me that perhaps I had displaced onto a fictional model what was an *instinctive* fear felt by northern women at the time. We were afraid of 'his' 'creeping' up to us from behind – I certainly was – yet how did we know he came from behind, since details of the attacks were only released after the man's arrest? I also discovered then that Sutcliffe was 'car mad' – that he spent his spare time playing with motors. *Shades of Grey* has a story called 'La Roue' ('The Wheel'), in which a man becomes fanatically fond of his car as a refuge against the 'predatoriness' of his wife and mother. Another story, 'The Immaculate Conception', is about a woman whom frustration and thwarted motherhood drive to compulsive and ultimately suicidal house-cleaning. This seemed to be what had happened to Sonia, Sutcliffe's wife. Reading descriptions of her behaviour, her way of dressing, what her house looked like, I recognised details I had *invented*. Is it that there are universal forms of behaviour which the 'imagination' perceives, or had I been driven to work on Sutcliffe because I somehow sensed that I had 'been there' already? If the latter, what does it mean about me? Or had I 'been there' for the same reasons that the Sutcliffes and Sonias of this world come into existence? Or again, are the types of displacements that lead to the double 'schizophrenias' of a Sutcliffe and a Sonia also present in anybody who strains under a *dual*, a *bilingual* situation? By 'dual', I mean that instead of being 'in control', having 'one being' which is French *or* English, working-class *or* middle-class, 'male' *or* female (*and* enjoys a 'proficiency' of some sort in the 'other' mode) you are – 'moitié-de-poulet', quoi.

*   *   *

Of Truth; 'Snakethinking'; and Safecracking

How to arrive at truth. The right relation to truth. The right image for truth. If you speak with bilingual tongue. But perhaps white woman always speaks with bilingual tongue. White woman speaks with forked tongue.

Create a field, perhaps. A field full of contradictions.

This first:

> There are phrases which help us not to admit we are lying: 'my privacy', 'nobody's business but my own' ...
> ... Does a life 'in the closet' – lying, perhaps of necessity, about ourselves to bosses, landlords, clients, colleagues, family, because the law and public opinion are founded on a lie – does this, can it, spread into private life, so that lying (described as *discretion*) becomes an easy way to avoid conflict or complication? can it become a strategy so ingrained that it is used even with close friends and lovers?[2]

Now for a bit of translation:

> Above all she remembered to distrust paradoxical thoughts. Because they are true serpents, the disciples of Milton's beautiful Snake, she knew something about it: there is a curve in their slimness which has always unaccountably seduced her; what held her was not the message but the enigma of its logic; and the enigma was how at a certain point in the speech what began as truth ended up as falsehood ...
> In the end this snakethinking sickened her. She felt that the paradox was only thinking through imitations of thought ...
> Thought she'd known for a long time that the secret of its seductiveness was perhaps nothing else but its secrecy. Because everything that is hidden, is seductive. And it is the oldest secret in the world, and it would long ago have ceased to be secret, if it wasn't being lost and hidden again every time.[3]

Both bits as a possible comment on the following supposedly bilingual image:

Craftmanship. Labour. Patience. But I don't get a crop. I don't have a birthright. More: I suddenly think as I look at myself writing sentences, forward, backward, no, not quite there, got to adjust them so the paragraph works, so that it should finally click, can't have that. Try this one. More like a burglar who's skilled at opening safes. Ear to the delicate clock. Listen to the faint whirring of the dents as you move from one to the other till the magic, the barely perceptible pause tells you

you've got the right number there. Next. And next. Till at the end of the day, oh wonder of wonders, you give a little shove, a little pull, and instead of all the sirens caught in the act race away like hell, the heavy door glides gracefully open. Yes. It has to do with theft: both in French and in English. Silence. Secrecy. Daring: the cracking of *safes* is full of risks. No violence, no thrusting or penetrating pens and what-nots (only an 'I' to add, can't do that in French, 'pens' + 'I' = One = safe identity), no rape of the virgin page, of the soft body of language pah pah pah. None of that. In any case, you know perfectly well that you're *also* the safe. You haven't got a wife to play that role for you.[4] But your ear, so attentive, the clock is like a bird to tame (plenty of time; I won't hurt you; relax). Every sound it makes you've got to interpret. And no two safes are alike. Not just because the codes and right and left are different in different countries, you don't drive on the same side of the road and driving-wheel and gears are on different sides, do you change hands when you write in French? Do you write English with your left hand? But because each is fitted in a different place, for a particular function.

Have I cracked this one? Yes. I see wads of notes, some typescript pages, perhaps a few banknotes. Yes, I have cracked it. Useful to have done so. But as soon as it clicked open, I realised that the lady of the house, canny lass that she is, had removed the valuables to some other hiding place. She only let me have a go at this one because she knew that what she truly treasures had been secreted away from it.

Notes

1. See 'Traduire', in *Des Femmes en Mouvement*, (mensuelle, no. 4, April 1978), p. 78.
2. Adrienne Rich, *On Lies, Secrets and Silence* (Virago, 1980), p. 190.
3. Hélène Cixous, *Limonade tout était si infini* (Editions des femmes, 1982). Needless to add, 'my' translation.
4. This obscure crack is levelled at a particularly objectionable French writer, Jean-Edern Hallier, who in his book, *L'Enlèvement*, which is full of the most violently misogynist images, boasts of having burgled his own wife's safe.

3

AT THE THRESHOLD OF THE SELF: WOMEN AND AUTOBIOGRAPHY

Linda Anderson

In his famous 'Preliminary Communication' on hysteria which he published with Breuer in 1893 and which laid the basis of all his future psychoanalytic work, Freud wrote that 'hysterics suffer mainly from reminiscences'.[1] This phrase marks an important stage in his understanding of the unconscious: the 'reminiscences' the hysteric suffers from are not conscious but repressed, mutely displaced across the body as symptom or illness. Freud found a meaning in the symptoms themselves – rather than merely the empirical evidence of illness – by replacing them by language. He discovered a way of opening up repressed memory through the mediation of psychoanalytic interpretation. Paradoxically, however, this approach to the unconscious could only be made by also moving away from the unconscious into language. Psychoanalysis could never fully represent the meaning of the unconscious, as Freud himself recognised; there would always be a point beyond which interpretation could not go, where the mind 'reaches down into the unknown'.[2] What psychoanalysis did was rather to follow the production of the meaning of the unconscious within language. This also suggests a very complicated sense of connection between past and present. Memories *become* speech: this means that their past meaning will be known only in terms of what they will become. Indeed, Freud came to believe that memories were never memories of actual events but phantasies, constructed out of wishes and their repression; in other words that they did not have an existence in reality outside their psychic function. The neurotic for Freud was someone who could not tell their own story. The story did not already exist, it had to be constructed. Psychoanalysis moved psychic life into a verbal and narrative dimension of time. It gave the self a history. What distinguished the neurotic was the experiencing of the present in terms of a repetition of the past, a collapsing of temporality into the simultaneity of present and past. 'Hysteria was linked to place,' Freud wrote.[3] Freud's project was to allow his patients to 'find a way out'[4] by liberating them through language into language and thus also into time.

Freud went on in his later work to relate hysteria to his theories of sexuality. Hysterical symptoms, like all neurotic symptoms for Freud, arose out of the conflict between instinctual impulses and their repression. But hysterical symptoms could be further analysed as the simultaneous and conflicting expression of 'two libidinal phantasies of an opposite sexual character'.[5] Suggesting that the hysterical attack was the unconscious representation of sexual activity, he wrote:

> Speaking as a whole, hysterical attacks, like hysteria in general, revive a piece of sexual activity in women which existed during their childhood and at that time revealed an essentially masculine character.[6]

The hysteric becomes someone for whom the Oedipal complex and the acquisition of sexual difference which that entails has been imperfectly resolved; who in attempting to occupy both the male and female positions refuses the ordering which it imposes. If, as Juliet Mitchell tells us, a person undergoes at the Oedipal moment 'the crucial acquisition of the story of his life',[7] then the hysteric is someone who cannot find his/her place within that particular story.

Initially, Freud did not associate hysteria exclusively with women. At the same time, though, the case studies that are used in *Studies on Hysteria* and the development of his understanding of it in terms of sexual identity point to its implicit definition as a form of female psychopathology. Indeed it could be argued that the claim for universality authorised certain kinds of blindness;

it allowed Freud to bring in his theories of sexuality without clearly foregrounding the significance of sexual difference. The hysteric, for Freud, was disturbed in her sexual identity, but what he fails to interrogate is the term female itself and the bias of his own viewpoint as male. Turning things round it could be suggested that Freud's linking of femininity with hysteria gives us an insight into the problem of femininity which Freud did not wholly intend: that women do not move simply into a female identity and role nor is that identity 'natural' or pre-given.

In recent years hysteria, and in particular Freud's most famous case study of a hysteric, 'Dora', have become an important focus for feminist discussion and revision.[8] In 1976 Hélène Cixous published her play based on Freud's account, *Portrait de Dora*, which was also performed in the same year.[9] The choice of dramatic form in place of Freud's narrative is itself an important part of her re-working. She undermines the authority of Freud's authorship and his single interpretation by introducing different voices and allowing for the gaps in understanding between them. The play also gives us a different mode of reality and a different use of language through associations and dreams as a way of opening into Dora's unconscious. By juxtaposing this with Freud's analytic interpretations she suggests how Dora's unconscious exceeds his scope. At the end of the play he is left literally speechless when Dora finishes the analysis and refuses to be contained by his interpretations of her. Freud has the power of writing but Dora walks out of the story. Her last words in the play are: 'Write ... That's not my affair' (p. 66). Freud can master the text but not her. He can take control by writing or rewriting the story, by producing a coherent account and thus attempting to repair the fragmentary nature of the analysis. What Hélène Cixous does is to open up the spaces and discontinuities again that he has attempted to close.

Cixous opposes Freud's version of opening up Dora through analysis by exploring a different kind of openness in her text. Dora is placed at a threshold through which she feels unable to pass:

> I can't keep myself away from this door – forever, I approach it, I linger in front of it, but I don't do it, I can't bring myself to go through it, I am full of memories and despair, and the strange thing

is that I could go through it but something is holding me back. (p. 31)

For Freud the 'key' is her acceptance of sexuality. 'Sexuality,' he wrote, 'is the key to the problem of the psychoneuroses and of the neuroses in general. No one who disdains the key will ever be able to unlock the door.'[10] But sexuality here means Dora experiencing herself as the object of male desire, that is being determined, defined by male desire just as she is by Freud's interpretation of her sexuality. What she is offered is really another form of closure; her role remains passive, her own desire dependent on her appropriation as erotic object.

Recent feminist readings of 'Dora' have challenged Freud's focus, his masculine gaze, and attempted to define a different economy of desire. What they have emphasised are certain crucial areas of silence in Freud's text created by the way he pushes to the margins both Dora's lesbian attachment to Frau K. and her relationship with her mother. Freud implicitly approves Dora's own rejection of her mother, and adds his own unflattering assessment of her: 'I was led to imagine her as an uncultivated woman and above all as a foolish one.'[11] Thus he fails to question what place this relationship occupies for Dora. Similarly he can only envisage Dora's desire for a woman occurring as a mimicry of male desire; the subject of desire presupposes a masculine subject and Dora therefore must be identifying with the man. According to Freud's theory the woman in the course of normal development represses her pre-Oedipal attachment to her mother, which he in any case conceptualises according to a male/female model; in taking on a feminine identity she abandons her mother, seeking to replace or to become her in relation to her father. For Freud, therefore, a woman's identification with and desire for the mother cannot exist in the same place. Sharon Willis in a very interesting discussion of 'Dora' takes up this point, first of all quoting Michèle Montrelay:

For the woman enjoys her body as she would the body of another. Every occurrence of a sexual kind happens to her as if it came from a feminine other, every occurrence is the fascinating actualisation of the femininity of all women, but also and above all, of the

57

mother. It is as if to 'become a woman', gave access to a *jouissance* of the body as feminine and/or maternal.

She then goes on to comment:

What is significant here is the idea of the persistence of a simultaneous identification and desire, and of femininity as constituted in an incessant process of repetition, reversal, and dispossession, dispersal across an 'other'.[12]

The woman is being seen within a different paradigm here as both self and other, both subject and object of desire; she recognises herself within an absence or a loss, in her resemblance to her mother from whom she is alienated. Instead of making the woman pass through the threshold into exile as Freud does, this different configuration of the female subject places her continually at a threshold, makes her herself a threshold. The process of becoming a subject, achieving autonomy in this view carries within itself as well a process of return to maternal origins. The return can never be completed, however; if it were the woman would be simply assimilated to the maternal body in a place outside language. But recognising within herself the process of return, her own interiority, she can constitute herself differently within the symbolic. Re-writing Freud we could say that the hysteric instead of 'suffering from reminiscences' lives the necessity of remembering, of gesturing towards her own origins in order not to forget. Hélène Cixous, talking about loss, suggests that the male mourns in order to get through loss. The woman, however, carries her loss within her and lives it endlessly. Hers is an 'open memory that ceaselessly makes way'.[13] This important phrase characterises a movement which is simultaneously forwards and backwards, outwards and inwards. It suggests the way memory can become self-creation.

Inevitably autobiography as the attempt to write the self, or give the self a narrative, is deeply bound up with these questions or questionings of identity. Recent work on it as a genre has incorporated the insights of psychoanalysis into the unconscious and language and has used them with great theoretical sophistication to turn the major assumption of autobiography back on itself. Georges Gusdorf, in an influential essay, notes that the autobiographer 'gives himself the job of narrating his own history; what he sets out to do is to reassemble the scattered elements of his individual life and to regroup them in a comprehensive sketch.'[14] The text, however, can never reproduce that intention since it necessarily substitutes a present reflection for the past event. James Olney makes the same point when he comments:

> In the act of remembering the past in the present, the autobiographer imagines into existence another person, another world, and surely it is *not* the same, in any real sense, as that past world that does not, under any circumstances, nor however much we may wish it, now exist.[15]

The autobiographer can never write the 'image-double'[16] of his life; instead in referring to himself he creates himself at every moment afresh within the text. What these critics are stressing is the tautological nature of autobiography; the idea that emerges in their work is that the autobiographical self is a fictional construct within the text which can neither have its origins anterior to the text nor indeed coalesce with its creator.

From our point of view while these theories interestingly engage with the idea of the past being displaced by language within the autobiographical narrative and thus make the link with psychoanalysis, what they fail to consider is how the writer, situated in langùage, is also inscribed in an order of sexual difference. Though the self may only exist as a story that can be told about the self, it is not necessarily the same story. It would be as wrong to see the production of autobiographical narratives as having no ideological significance – no basis within nor reference to history or culture – as it would psychoanalysis itself. It is necessary to take into account the fact that the woman who attempts to write herself is engaged by the nature of the activity itself in re-writing the stories that already exist about her since by seeking to publicise herself she is violating an important cultural construction of her femininity as passive or hidden. She is resisting or changing what is known about her. Her place within culture, the place from which she writes, is produced by difference and produces difference. The myth of the self which recent theorists have questioned may not be present for her in the same way; it is more difficult for her to believe in a self that can exist before writing, a self that is unified and continuous. Autobiography may selfconsciously exist for her as an alternative place of identification. This means that there may be a greater formal awareness in her writing, an emphasis on the self-reflexiveness of writing, the idea of the self as written. In writing herself the woman is also reaching into writing and her story will more obviously be informed by a dynamics of self-becoming. But there is no point of arrival; she can neither transcend herself nor attain to some authentic fullness of being. It is a dynamic which is shadowed by loss, which exists between loss, absence and what might be. As we have seen in psychoanalytic terms the woman's presence encircles an absence and her writing, too, exists at a threshold, referring back in a constant process of coming into being.

The diary is a good starting-point from which to consider these ideas because of the way its importance is bound up with the problems of authorship for women. Historically it has offered the woman the possibility of laying claim to writing while allaying the anxieties of actual publication. Poised ambivalently between private and public statement, it can also be seen as a process, rooted in the private dimension of living which does not take its goal or form from its status as social and cultural artifact. It allows the woman to remain hidden while providing her with a place to actualise her interiority, create herself for an 'other', even if that 'other' is also herself. For Virginia Woolf who clearly did establish herself as a writer in other forms the diary still remained important and she suggests that the diary's privacy and seeming ephemerality could be alternatively understood as an experimental possibility. She recorded in her own diary that

> there looms ahead of me the shadow of some kind of form which a diary might attain to. I might in the course of time learn what it is that one can make of this loose, drifting material of life; finding another use for it than the use I put it to, so much more consciously and scrupulously, in fiction. What sort of diary should I like mine to be? Something loose knit and yet not slovenly, so elastic that it will embrace any thing, solemn, slight or beautiful that comes into my mind. I should like it to resemble some deep old desk, or capacious hold-all, in which one flings a mass of odds and ends without

looking them through. I should like to come back, after a year or two, and find that the collection had sorted itself and refined itself and coalesced, as such deposits so mysteriously do, into a mould, transparent enough to reflect the light of our life, and yet steady, tranquil compounds with the aloofness of a work of art.[17]

While the diary for many writers can be regarded as a symptom of restriction, giving a provisional voice to women who were denied confident access to public expression, here Virginia Woolf is consciously going back to it for its figuring of personal space. Her desk, like her 'room of one's own', seems expressive of the need to define that space whatever its limits. Significantly, what she stresses about her desk is its depth, suggesting an unexplored interiority and spaciousness. The diary's formlessness, its lack of continuity, its random breaks and its joining up of different moments and areas of experience – its denial of narrative – becomes the most appropriate form for a shifting, questing subjectivity. It is interesting that the form remains as potential – 'there looms ahead of me' – present and yet also absent, a 'shadow'. It is a container, a 'mould', which is also not there, 'invisible'. It is also worth noting that the creativity Virginia Woolf imagines happens passively without the assertion or even presence of herself as creator. She herself remains withdrawn, invisible.

For Alice James the diary was also a kind of invisible writing, though what Woolf transformed into a modernist quest for aesthetic release from personality was more clearly marked by repression, by social and psychological deprivation, in Alice James's case. She began to keep her diary in 1889 at the age of forty and though she may have supported the idea of eventual, posthumous publication, it was not published in her lifetime, nor did she ever seek publication in any other way. Only her nurse and her companion Katharine Loring knew about the existence of the diary; her brother Henry had to wait until her death to discover it and to become fully aware of his sister's literary aspirations. By the time she began to write her diary, Alice James was firmly established in her role as invalid having been unable to reconcile her ambitions to achieve intellectually and artistically – which would have meant competing with her brothers William and Henry – with the different 'feminine' expectations of her to be selfless and 'good'. Illness removed her from the conflict as well as at a deeper level giving expression to it, enabling her in her passivity to retain the ambiguous power of moral superiority. Jean Strouse, her biographer, comments on how from her position as invalid she cultivated a detachment which

> enabled her to submit and resist at the same time. It was as if she ceded her body to the 'feminine' principle of frailty and submission, while cultivating with her mind a 'masculine' strength and indifference to pain.[18]

It is this same quality of detachment which we can perceive in her writing: it hovers somewhere a little above the needs and conflicts to which it is a response offering a precarious, willed transcendence. This is her first entry:

> I think that if I get into the habit of writing a bit about what happens, or rather doesn't happen, I may lose a little of the sense of loneliness and desolation which abides with me. My circumstances allowing of nothing but the ejaculation of one-syllabled reflections, a written monologue by that most interesting being, myself, may have its yet to be discovered consolations. I shall at least have it all my own way and it may bring relief as an outlet to that geyser of emotions, sensations, speculations and reflections which ferments perpetually within my poor old carcass for its sins; so here goes, my first Journal![19]

The central act of self-naming in this passage, the underlining of the word 'myself', also forms a focus of anxiety. The phrase preceding it, 'that most interesting being', holds this dangerous act of self-assertion in check by drawing attention to it and ironically undercutting it. Similarly the turmoil of her emotions and thoughts, imaged in a way which suggests her repressed creative potentiality is being both expressed and expelled; it poses a threat to her physical weakness which she must, for her own mental survival, struggle to protect and preserve as weakness. The frail 'feminine' body which Jean Strouse refers to runs the risk of being overwhelmed by undisciplined energy and the effort of control is apparent in her slightly mocking self-consciousness. She can break through restrictions, both real and self-imposed, to 'have it her own way' in her writing; the diary,

in other words, can be a space of freedom and potentiality which she has created in defiance. But there is another need too – for validation and acceptance. In speaking to herself as imagined other, in writing a monologue as she says, she is also acting out her need to be heard and this to some extent thwarts her writing, making her conceal emotionally as much as she reveals.

In a later entry in the same year she turned towards the past for release into a more unrestricted sense of being. It is perhaps not insignificant that this passage follows on from some slightly uncomfortable remarks about marriage:

> I have seen so little that my memory is packed with little bits which have not been wiped out by great ones, so that it all seems like a reminiscence and as I go along the childish impressions of light and colour come crowding back into my mind and with them the expectant, which then palpitated within me, lives for a ghostly moment.[20]

What she is doing here is finding a place inside herself which is also outside the roles offered to her by her society. Her language evokes sensations, experiences of light and colour which are non-verbal or even pre-verbal. Memory works upon consciousness by dissolving or fragmenting it into indeterminacy, loosening the boundaries between past and present: 'it all seems like a reminiscence'. She becomes a subject in process, and the time of writing is lost in a non-teleological structuring of past and future. Looking backwards she also looks forward expectantly; she creates an intense internal space, with its own interior dynamic for her writing. Her use of the word 'palpitated' gives a physicality to the disembodied 'ghostly' moment, simultaneously enclosing it within her with its metaphorical associations with gestation, and giving it linguistic flesh, outer shape and form. She is finding a point of balance between inner and outer, a momentary fullness, as memory 'crowds' her mind, pushing her at the same time into and out of being.

We can perceive this same pattern of retrospection, memory, breaking the surface in what is also a movement of recovery in the work of a contemporary writer, Kate Millett. In many ways her situation and her reasons for turning to autobiographical writing are very different from Alice James's. She did not lack access to publication in the same way; indeed, it was precisely her success, which amounted to notoriety, after the publication of *Sexual Politics* which made autobiography an imperative for her as a different place of identification. What Kate Millett experienced as published author was an inability to reconcile inner and outer experience. The publicity not only destroyed her privacy but also seemed to negate her own inner experience. In *Flying* and *Sita* she interrogates the boundary between inner and outer, producing as she does so narratives which in their concentration on momentary impressions and their disjointedness have much of the feel of a diary. Both books seem both to chart a process of near breakdown and also to defend Millett against it. 'If I scribble something,' she writes in *Sita*, 'I am writing rather than falling apart.'[21] Kate Millett is able through autobiography to expose her vulnerability, dissolving the public, assured persona – the author she has become – in the experience of private pain, seeking through the experience of pain and loss a different place from which to write. Trying to explain in *Flying* why she decided to 'treat my own existence as documentary', she notes:

> There are many reasons why I shouldn't have. Among them some credit is due to common sense. I did realize my scheme was in bad taste, a divulgence superfluous even before one considers its impropriety. I have a powerful respect for the pleasing, reasonable dishonesty of civilized discretion. One reason I thought it worth doing is because I'm fairly sure that had someone once tried to tell me all this I would have been interested. Especially if I had heard it while there was still time. One's impressions during such an experience, the bits of what an observer sees and thinks then – recording them, even if they were my own, might, I hoped, just conceivably have some marginal value. I'm still not sure.[22]

Inevitably this anxious attempt at self-justification ends in uncertainty, she is caught here within contradictory pressures. Having to transgress the codes of what it is acceptable to reveal in order to explore those previously silent, unrecorded areas of experience, what she discovers can only be defined as 'superfluous' and 'marginal' when brought back into the public again. Existing outside those codes it cannot be validated within them. Her writing enacts a continual fracturing of its own surface, a breaking into disorder and uncertainty, as a way of searching behind the formal structure, the accepted patterns of order and significance. She breaks definitions, breaks down, in order to move towards a different kind of definition, one which can include hesitancy and vulnerability, which continually undermines its own authority as statement.

In a sense women's autobiography is both a reaching towards the possibility of saying 'I' and towards a form in which to say it. Writing is a quest, a process. 'Searching I write' Christa Wolf has noted in an essay appropriately entitled 'Interview with Myself'.[23] In her novels which seem to hover on a borderline between fact and fiction she writes into the space of what she has called in another essay the 'remembered future':[24]

Writing means making things large. Pulling ourselves together, let's see her writ large. One's wishes are only what one is capable of. Thus her deep and persistent wish guarantees the secret existence of her work: this *long and neverending journey towards oneself.*
The difficulty of saying 'I'.[25]

This is from the end of Christa Wolf's novel, *The Quest for Christa T.*, which records the narrator's memories of her dead friend, Christa T. and her attempt to find some pattern and significance in them and in her friend's life. Increasingly the distinctions between character and narrator become difficult to sustain – what is unknown is both an external and an internal goal of knowledge. The narrator's journey into the past becomes also the discovery of the unrealised potentiality of her friend's life which can only be made real in the attempt to write about it. The novel is both about loss and a recovery through writing and it is the ache towards, the process of writing which connects the two states, just as it connects the narrator with her shadow self, Christa T.

It would be possible within this context to see all Virginia Woolf's work, both fiction and non-fiction, as the exploration of the self as absent, as a space in which to create herself. She was well aware, for instance, of the problems of writing autobiography. 'One of the memoir writer's difficulties,' she observed in 'A Sketch of the Past', 'is that they leave out the person to whom things happened ... So they say: "This is what happened": but they do not say what the person was like to whom it happened.'[26] In a letter to her friend Ethel Smythe she also made the comment that 'there's never been a woman's autobiography'.[27] Conventional autobiography or memoir to which she refers in 'A Sketch of the Past' which takes the external events of a life as its focus and principle of organisation must by its very nature be alien or unavailable to women. Within such accounts, therefore, it may be the woman who is the missing person.

In *A Room of One's Own* Virginia Woolf enacted the reinstating of herself as woman by writing a biography for someone who had been missed out, who does not exist. Her invention of a life for Shakespeare's sister is in part her whimsical comment on the plight of the woman artist: it is a way of speculating about the internal and external pressures which silenced the woman of genius and deprived her of a place in history. But her creation of Shakespeare's sister is also Virginia Woolf's way of making the silence speak, of giving body to the absence and loss which is felt when we look for a female literary tradition, when we 'think back through our mothers'.[28] Shakespeare's sister is Woolf's incarnation of female creativity; she is the bringing into being of woman's creative presence. In this way she is also an act of self-creation, a finding within herself of the sources of creativity with which to combat the loss she encounters when she looks outwardly for a female literary tradition.

In an earlier work, her unpublished 'Journal of Mistress Joan Martyn' which was written in 1906, Virginia Woolf had in a similar way experimented with a form of biography which enacts the discovery of woman as a person missing from history.[29] Joan Martyn's biography – this time contained in the form of a journal, itself, of course, written by Virginia Woolf – is framed by her absence within the official historical records of the period which supposedly belong to the fifteenth century. Virginia Woolf invents as a way of introducing the journal a female historian, Rosamund Meridew, who is looking for documents relating to the land tenure system of medieval England. In many ways Woolf's surrogate, she is in conflict with orthodox historical research and defends her right to speculate about and imaginatively recreate the social and domestic life which finds no place in the historical documents she is concerned with. The journal itself is thus reached through a system of framing devices. It is appropriately brought to light by a woman's search for another hidden and overlooked version of history. It is also the discovery of one woman by another, implying a different sense of ancestry, a female line of descent. Structurally the journal is to be found on the inside. We pass through the external layers to this internal space and the immediate experience of the journal and the subjective voice that speaks to us through it. Lost in history, Joan Martyn is only in the process of coming into being to herself; hers is a life which is being created through her own dimly realised internal experiences. Throughout the journal there is a sense of yearning for something submerged or not yet attained:

> Yet what it is I want, I cannot tell, although I crave for it, and in some secret way, expect it. For often and oftener as time goes by, I find myself suddenly halting in my walk, as though I were stopped by a strange new look upon the surface of the land which I know so well. It hints at something; but it is gone before I know what it means; it half frightens you, and yet it beckons. (pp. 265-6)

The process of discovery of this hidden life, which we as readers have been led through, is paralleled within the diary by this movement towards the unknown. The female self exists as a potentiality which has never fully come into being. Joan Martyn dies when she is thirty, when she is on the point of losing her name and her definable place in history to a husband. At the same time, though, what Virginia Woolf has done is also to transform the loss of Joan Martyn into an eloquent presence both through the journal itself and Rosamund Meridew's resurrection of it.

When Virginia Woolf was writing her own autobiographical sketch, 'A Sketch of the Past', in 1939, she was simultaneously engaged in writing her biography of Roger Fry. Her own memoir is written, therefore, in the spaces that can be created, the time that can be spared, from that much more conventional and impersonal record of a life. Her own sketch registers her sense of frustration and constraint about the Fry work. It becomes also a way of resisting the patterning of the biography, a breaking away into her own sense of personal freedom. In opposition to the coherence and wholeness that she wants to achieve in the Fry biography there is in her own sketch an acceptance of randomness and fragmentation. 'These distracted and disconnected thoughts', she calls the sketch at one point (p. 111). The sketch serves as notes towards something unwritten: it becomes a search for a form to express the inexpressible, what is unknown or forgotten or in continual movement about herself. The diary form which she adopts, the introduction of dates and a sense of the present moment, gives her, as she says, 'a platform to stand on' (p. 86) but it is also a deliberate attempt to give expression to her sense of ephemerality: 'What I write today I should not write in a year's time' (p. 87). The past cannot be disentangled from the present from which it takes its shape and meaning. 'I make it real by putting it into words,' she writes (p. 84). Remembering, opening her writing to disjointedness and fragmentation, becomes part of an effort to achieve wholeness. She writes about the past in order to create a sense of identity for herself in the present: 'I write this partly in order to recover my sense of the present by getting the past to shadow this broken surface' (p. 115).

The present and the past can be alternately shadow and substance for Virginia Woolf, the existence of each being reflected against the absence of the other. The present can seem unreal because of its lack of depth, its lack of contact with her unconscious. Thus her sense of frustration with the Fry work. However her memories can also seem insubstantial, lacking reference to anything 'real'. She is disturbed that her memory of her mother, who died when she was fourteen and which, as she says 'obsessed' her up to the time that she wrote *To the Lighthouse* and which dominates this sketch too, can now only float within the space of her own mind:

> For what reality can remain real of a person who dies forty-four years ago at the age of forty-nine without leaving a book, or a picture, or any piece of work – apart from the three children who now survive and the memory of her that remains in their minds? There is the memory; but there is nothing to check that memory by; nothing to bring it to ground with. (p. 99)

In an interesting earlier passage she had attempted to trace her first memory and in trying to locate her origins describes the point at which her sense of herself merges with that of her mother. The first memory

> was of red and purple flowers on a black ground – my mother's dress; and she was sitting either in a train or in an omnibus, and I was on her lap. I therefore saw the flowers she was wearing very close; and can still see purple and red and blue. I think against the black; they must have been anemones, I suppose. Perhaps we were going to St Ives; more probably, for from the light it must have been evening we were coming back to London. But it is more convenient artistically to suppose that we were going to St Ives, for that will lead to my other memory, which also seems to be my first memory and in fact it is the most important of all my memories. If life has a base that it stands upon, if it is a bowl that one fills and fills and fills – then my bowl without doubt stands upon this memory. It is of lying half asleep half awake in bed in the nursery at St Ives. It is of hearing the waves breaking, one, two, one, two and sending a splash of water over the beach; and then breaking one, two, one, two behind a yellow blind. It is of hearing the blind draw its little acorn across the floor as the wind blew the blind out. It is of lying and hearing this splash and seeing this light and feeling it is almost impossible that I should be here; of feeling the purest ecstacy I can conceive. (pp. 74-5)

These 'colour and sound' memories, as Virginia Woolf calls them (p. 77), connected to the experience of closeness to her mother's body, foreshorten the perspective, closing the gap in time through the representation of physical proximity. This memory leads into another which metaphorically also seems to recall the mother, suggesting the 'oceanic' feelings of oneness with her that we would associate with the pre-Oedipal phase. Here desire and identity meet in 'ecstacy', an ecstacy which is both of union and separateness.

Having once felt enclosed by her mother who was the 'whole' (p. 96), Virginia Woolf encircles her in her writing. The image she uses of the bowl suggests this simultaneous fullness and emptiness, a completeness and autonomy achieved through aesthetic form which is structured around an absence; but an absence which can also be full. Her memories of her mother both contain her and are contained by her. This ambivalence is returned to in her memory of her mother's death:

It was sunset and the great glass dome at the end of the station was blazing with light. It was glowing yellow and red and the iron girders made a pattern across it. I walked along the platform gazing with rapture at this magnificent blaze of colour and the train slowly steamed into the station. It impressed and exalted me. It was so vast and so fiery red. The contrast of that blaze of magnificent light with the shrouded and curtained rooms at Hyde Park Gate was so intense. Also it was partly that my mother's death unveiled and intensified, made me suddenly develop perceptions, as if a burning glass had been laid over what was shaded and dormant. (p. 108)

The words 'unveiled and intensified' precisely express the simultaneity of loss and creativity since they can be read in two senses; either the memory of her mother's death becomes present for her or the death releases her into a new intensity of perception and being. Both meanings are there, just as the light, the intense brilliance, is dependent on the shade, the darkness of absence. For Virginia Woolf the act of remembering and of writing come together. By remembering she creates the possibility of her own writing, endlessly discovering herself within loss at what Hélène Cixous has called 'the turning point of making'.[30] Using the imagery which Virginia Woolf herself used in *A Room of One's Own* we could say that she refused the choice of either being locked in or being locked out (p. 24). She returns us to Freud with a renewed sense that the threshold is not hesitation, not a refusal to become part of a different story, but its own beginning.

Notes

1. *Studies on Hysteria*, in *The Complete Works of Freud* (standard edn, Hogarth Press, London, 1955), Vol. II, p. 7. All further references to Freud are to this edition.
2. Ibid., *The Interpretation of Dreams*, vol. V, p. 525.
3. Quoted by Julia Kristéva in 'Women's Time', *Signs*, 7 (1981), 13-35, p. 15.
4. Freud, *Studies on Hysteria*, p. 17.
5. Freud, 'Hysterical Phantasies and Their Relation to Bisexuality', vol. IX, p. 165.
6. Freud, 'Some General Remarks on Hysterical Attacks', vol. IX, p. 234.

7. Juliet Mitchell, *Psychoanalysis and Feminism* (Penguin, Harmondsworth, 1975), p. 14.
8. See Jacqueline Rose, ' "Dora" – Fragment of an Analysis', *M/F* 2(1978), 5-21; Suzanne Gearhart, 'The Scene of Psychoanalysis: The Unanswered Questions of Dora', *Diacritics*, 9 (1979) 114-26; Toril Moi, 'Representation of Patriarchy: Sexuality and Epistemology in Freud's Dora', *Feminist Review*, 9 (1981) 60-74; The whole volume of *Diacritics*, Spring (1983).
9. (Editions des femmes, Paris 1976). English translation published in *Benmussa Directs* (Clader, London, 1979). All references are to this translation.
10. Freud, 'Fragment of An Analysis of a Case of Hysteria', vol. VII, p. 115.
11. Ibid., p. 20.
12. Freud, 'A Symptomatic Narrative', *Diacritics*, Spring (1983), 46-60, pp. 55-6.
13. Hélène Cixous, 'Castration or Decapitation', *Signs*, 7 (1981), 41-55, p. 54.
14. Georges Gusdorf, 'Conditions and Limits of Autobiography', in *Autobiography: Essays Theoretical and Critical* ed. James Olney (Princeton University Press, Princeton, N.J., 1980), p. 35.
15. James Olney, 'Some Versions of Memory/Some Versions of *Bios*: The Ontology of Autobiography', in *Autobiography*, p. 241.
16. Georges Gusdorf, 'Conditions and Limits of Autobiography', p. 40.
17. *A Writer's Diary*, ed. Leonard Woolf (Granada, St Albans, 1973), p. 23.
18. Jean Strouse, *Alice James: A Biography* (Bantam, New York, 1982), p. 136.
19. *The Diary of Alice James*, ed. Leon Edel (Penguin, Harmondsworth, 1982), p. 25 (31 May 1889).
20. Ibid., p. 34 (16 June 1889).
21. Kate Millett, *Sita* (Virago, London, 1977), p. 60.
22. Kate Millett, *Flying* (Hart-Davis MacGibbon, St Albans, 1975), pp. 81-2.
23. Christa Wolf, 'Interview with Myself 1966', in *The Reader and the Writer* (Seven Seas Books, Berlin, 1977), p. 76.
24. Christa Wolf, 'The Reader and the Writer', p. 210.
25. Christa Wolf, *Quest for Christa T* (Virago, London, 1982), p. 174.
26. Virginia Woolf, in *Moments of Being* (Granada, St Albans, 1978), p. 75.
27. *The Letters of Virginia Woolf* (Chatto & Windus, London, 1980), vol. VI, p. 453 (24 December 1940).
28. Virginia Woolf, *A Room of One's Own* (The Hogarth Press, London, 1967), p. 114.
29. 'Virginia Woolf's "The Journal of Mistress Joan Martyn"', ed. Susan M. Squier and Louise A. DeSalvo, *Twentieth Century Literature*, 25 (1979), 237-69.
30. Hélène Cixous, 'Castration or Decapitation', p. 47.

4

VOICES ARE WILD

Michelene Wandor

Sometimes when I am reading a poem, one of my own poems, at a poetry reading, something odd happens. Time and place retreat for a moment. I can hear my voice saying the words, but I can't feel any conviction behind the words. I am absolutely certain that everyone in the audience is bored out of their minds, and I have a very strong impulse to stop reading the poem, look up at the audience and say, 'God, that's boring. I'll read another one.' Then again, at another reading, I can be reading the self-same poem, and I have a very strong sense of the whole of me speaking through the sounds my voice is making, I know exactly where I am, I am absolutely certain that the audience can hear every syllable and nuance, and there is no distance between us at all, except the sound of my voice and the silence of theirs.

If I was acting a part in a play, I would put the first experience down to a lapse in concentration, a wandering away of my attention. But when I am reading a poem which I've written, I am not acting a part. I am me, speaking words which I have constructed into a poem and which is not-me. Theatrical performance is often fetishised as being somehow present in the instant of communication between performers and audience, as suspended between them, as intangible, as something that makes the drama unique as an art form. Of course there is some truth in that. The act of speech in public, of public speech, has a character which is different from personal conversation, and is different again from the speech-less act of writing. I'm linking theatre with poetry not just because of the shared performance aspects of both, but also because plays and poetry have been my main chosen forms of fiction in the past fifteen years, and both are built in various ways around the notion and the reality of 'voice'. Or 'voices'. I don't mean by this the conventional mystical notion of a literary voice which is entirely mysterious; I mean something much more complex, and something which has come more and more clearly into focus for me over the past three or four years. It is something upon which I now base my solo poetry readings (though they are far more than 'readings'), and it is something I try and come to terms with retrospectively, by re-reading things I've written over the years, trying to understand exactly what they are, 'who' wrote them, and why they take the form they do. That is what I want to explore here but I want also to preface it with an important word of cautionary warning.

You should be very careful indeed about taking anything any writer says about her/his fiction as gospel. You can be certain that any writer who rabbits on about the 'truth' is lying. The writing of fiction is, after all, the act of creating a construct which may be rooted in material conditions, may be traceable to certain sources and influences, but it will be a fantasy and imaginative construct which has no absolute material correlative in empirically verifiable reality. In other words, it will be a pack of lies. But what an exciting and invigorating pack of lies it can be. And I say that as a socialist and as a feminist. Particularly as a socialist and a feminist. Here, of course, I am beginning to talk about sets of political ideas and practices which have influenced me. I am jumping ahead too fast. Suffice it to say that I hope that everything here is in some way illuminating about the process of writing, but cannot really act as either a judgement on (say) my poetry, nor necessarily be the final word (words) on what it means. I can say what I think something I've written means to me, but I am very dependent (and frantically curious) on my audience (readers, listeners) to say what it means to them. I cannot legislate for the myriad meanings a piece of writing can produce. I cannot tell you how to 'read' what I write. I can only try and explain something of how I read what I have written.

The beginning of this concern to understand 'voice' lies in a piece of work I began in 1977 – though I was not aware of the concern at the time. At the end of the 1960s I picked up a second-hand copy of Elizabeth Barrett Browning's poetry. I flipped through it, and began ploughing my way through her long verse-novel 'Aurora Leigh'. It was terribly hard going and I have to admit I gave up well before the end. Then, in 1976 for some reason which I cannot now remember, I went back to it. I have a feeling that it may have been because I was re-reading a very excellent American feminist anthology, *Woman in Sexist Society*, edited by Vivian Gornick and Barbara Moran. This book was first published in 1971, and although I had read it avidly then, it was one of those books I would occasionally pick up and dip into. In it there is a marvellous essay by Elaine Showalter on Victorian women writers, and in it she mentions and quotes from 'Aurora Leigh'. I think that spurred me on to return to the original and work through to the end. I may say in passing that the work of feminist literary historians and critics has been of very great importance to me in providing a sense that others are interested in the same material, from different, and always illuminating perspectives.

This time I worked my way through the poem, and decided that I wanted to dramatise it. There were some reasons for this which I could articulate to myself: first, to make something difficult and important more accessible. Second, as part of my ongoing work of dramatising, adapting, basing plays, etc. on other texts. Third, the decision to dramatise the poem into a verse-play meant that I was having to write theatrical verse myself, and verse in the style of Elizabeth Barrett Browning, Victorian iambic pentameter. These reasons are not necessarily in order of precedence. Underneath them was something else. In working with a text, in literally taking it apart and then putting it together again, I establish an incredible intimacy with the words and the literary structure itself. At the same time I have enormous power, since I am in complete charge of the reconstruction. A complex dialogue is going on. There is the objective dialogue across time, of one woman writer working with another woman writer's text. But there is also something more difficult to define, and that is the communication between voices, between choices of word and image and phrase and content and emphasis; the process is one of exchange, translation and, above all, transformation. The transformation of one kind of text into another (verse into play), and in this way making the original come to life again in an original form. The ambiguity of the word 'original' here is intended.

When a new edition of 'Aurora Leigh' came out in 1978, my dramatisation was already finished. Cora Kaplan's superb introduction to the poem was very illuminating about a number of things, but she also pin-pointed something I was beginning to think about, which relates to the taboo on the publicly heard power of women's voices. Cora Kaplan comments:

> The taboo, it is stronger than prejudice, against women's entry into public discourse as speakers or writers, was in grave danger of being definitively broken in the mid-nineteenth century as more and more educated, literate women entered the arena as imaginative writers, social critics and reformers.[1]
> Public writing and public speech, closely allied, were both real and symbolic acts of self-determination for women.[2]

This has exact and direct bearing on one of the reasons why it is particularly problematic for women to engage seriously as playwrights. It is in the nature of drama that it is publicly presented, before a live audience. It is in the nature of playwrighting that the playwright is responsible for the text, and for the words that others speak. A kind of puppet mistress, perhaps, who creates an imaginative world, and then controls the whole of the speech and action in it, and literally dictates the words that others speak. I could hold forth at great length about this – indeed I have elsewhere[3] – and I mention it here because in focusing (without pre-planning, it just seems to have 'happened') on poetry and plays I seem to have lumbered myself with, at one and the same time, before your very eyes, the most public and the most private of literary utterances, and to be taking on the most public and private of associations with the power of the voice.

As well as this, I write critically about the theatre, and currently edit a series of annual anthologies of plays by women. My voices have thus spread across different kinds of genre, and give me different kinds of problems and satisfactions. It is on the matter of the kind of satisfaction (I hesitate to call it unity, or wholeness, because it is both more exciting and fragile than that, and anyway I don't like simple definitions or appeal to theory as the only way to explain what and why I write) which I referred to in the second paragraph of this piece, that I want to expand.

I started writing seriously in about 1968–69. It took a few years before I could recognise to myself that I was a professional writer, that I earned my living from writing. My beginnings as a writer were marked by a mixture of great personal turmoil and equally great political excitement. This was already reflected (I see now) in a division between genres. The personal turmoil was reflected in the fiction – the poetry and plays – the political excitement of feminism and socialism – in an applied form in journalism (theatre, book, film reviews) and in a more direct form in an attempt to write pieces of polemic, political analysis – very raw indeed, but the space where the political ideas themselves could flex. Looking back, there is what might appear to be a kind of literary schizophrenia, but I know it was the same person writing. Here, as an example, since the poetry is much more interesting than the reviews, is the beginning of one poem, with no title:

> ripping the skin off a dead rabbit
> but the image may disgust you;
> it is an attempt, in the light of –
> what I cannot send, and what
> is mislaid – to fathom whether it
> is a question of dredging the guts
> in the knowledge of a new
> generation; a new, re-generation;
> whether it is even worth
> speculation on the thory of the
> image.[4]

I can't say what the occasion was that prompted the poem; but it seems to me now precisely about (well, imprecisely, but certainly 'about') one of the things that has been absolutely no problem at all to me over the years, but which constantly seems to cause problems for aesthetes and politicos alike. That is the relationship in practice, in the precisions of an actual piece of writing, of the politics and art in the writer's head. To make a crude generalisation (which like all generalisations holds in general, and not for every single individual), most feminists and socialists don't seem interested in my more 'abstract' or 'experimentally' structured, non-narrative fiction, and the gentlemen (sic) who run theatres and poetry establishments fasten on to the more overt bits of evidence of feminism in my fiction and disregard the rest. The irony is, of course, that it is the politics that either pleases or bothers both sides of this equation, and the 'art' or the aesthetics, the excitement of what a writer (me) does with language, that seems to get lost – or be insufficiently appreciated.

Up till the end of 1971, most of the poems I wrote were dense, allusive, difficult to grasp (difficult for me to grasp often), and I think now, retrospectively, very exciting. I actually had far more in common with the men who were working with formal experimentation, and things like concrete poetry, than I did with my feminist and socialist sisters, with whom I was about to transform the world. There was on the Left, and in feminism as part of the radical landscape, a deep and hypocritical suspicion of the so-called individual 'bourgeois' arts, even though most of those scoffing at the moribundity of poetry were either writing their closet novels or reading Mills & Boon, and probably both. This is not to denigrate that contradiction, but to point to a radical set of principles which in public said that all art should be useful and instrumental for political struggle in an explicit way, and in private

> dance like fury to Stones
> raping words, to Rod Stewart piggery,
> and allow the moribund bits of them
> at their need for rhythm.[5]

There is already a difference between those two poems quoted. The first was written in 1971, the second in 1974. By 1974, when I was very heavily involved with Marxist and feminist study groups, was doing an MA in the Sociology of Literature, and having to earn my living from journalism, the writing of fiction was beginning to take a brief back-seat. The idea that the only justification that fiction had was if it was useful for political struggle and accessible to large numbers of people, was beginning to get to me. The poetry – such as I wrote – became more superficially 'available'. The words made sense like sentences do, it was no longer just a series of powerful and painful images and snippets of ideas yoked together in open form. In order to give these poems some kind of tang for myself, some of them took on a polemical and satirical air. In a small group of poems aspects of the political process itself became the subject of the poem, in the sense of that being what the poem was about. So 'June 1974'[6] was about the philistinism of right-on politicos towards art (as I felt it), and was directly prompted by a woman who made a throwaway remark to the effect that 'all poetry is moribund'. A decade later I learned that her greatest ambition at university was to be a novelist. Never mind. But it hurt at the time. Another poem, 'London airport',[7] written in 1973, was an attempt to bring the heady and exhilarating illuminations of feminist critiques of the family to bear on the pain of sending my children on holiday to their father. And it is also about ways in which poetry tries (or has tried) to deal with emotion and ideas at the same time. In another way – given my current pre-occupation – it can be seen as a piece of fiction in which the different voices of poetic and political discourse come together, and the language reflects that quite deliberately.

There. I have uttered the word. 'Discourse'. It is possible that in some readers' minds the word 'voice' translates itself as 'discourse'. That's OK. I have nothing against the word. On occasions I find it useful. And I shall use it now as a way of approaching a difficulty, a contradiction. I mentioned earlier how important I have found the work of feminist literary critics and historians, (I suppose I'm one myself, and I certainly think *my* work is important . . .) But seriously. I also have myself found both tremendous excitement and frustration with reading and coming to grips with theory. My first encounters with Marx were agony and rewarding. Ditto Althusser. Since then I have dipped and darted around various real, but also fashionable, theories as they have come and gone.

Some bits of some theory I find impossible to understand. Some annoy me, for reasons I don't quite comprehend. But the play of logic and argument in good and exciting theoretical writing gives me a great buzz. It gives me – the currently fashionable word in theoretical circles – 'pleasure'. But I knew I loved theory before 'pleasure' became an object for the survey of radical theorists. So I have an ambiguous relationship towards those whose primary practice is working with, and transforming theory. I admire it and get a huge amount from it. But I am also often suspicious that those whose work primarily focuses on the criticism and theorisation of other people's work, have contempt for the process of fiction-writing itself (ironic, really, since theorists are also writers themselves, even if sometimes only part-time ones), and that even very sophisticated thinkers (and this includes feminists as well as socialists and others) have a real block about recognising (refuse to recognise?) the fact that the writing of fiction is (a) a profession; (b) a craft; (c) the production of an artefact which can be subjected to a number of different responses and analyses; (d) something which provides cathartic, therapeutic, transformatory and no doubt other adjectival, experiences for both writer and reader. For example, while the relationship between form and a particular social formation (see, I remember that from my early 1970s Marxism) is fascinating and important (i.e. the circumstances of the development of naturalism in theatre in the late nineteenth century, for example) for the writer her/himself, the choices can never be fully and completely consciously articulated. You may think you know why you have 'chosen' to work with a particular form, but there are likely to be all sorts of subconscious reasons which cannot be understood until well afterwards. I am always very sceptical indeed about polemical calls for 'a new form', for prescriptive statements (which often do come from critics and theorists) about how fiction 'should' be written, since there is always a limit to the choices which can be consciously made. There are always cultural and individual voices which speak through the language one uses in a way which is not thought. It is like certain kinds of basic physical reflex, where we walk without thinking (consciously), and where we write or speak in the same way. The point is not a blanket dismissal of the 'old' in favour of the 'new', but a recognition of the moment in one's writing process where the 'thinking' voice which plans, analyses and tries to maintain control, is in dialogue with the voice that speaks unbidden.

In the middle of the 1970s my 'thinking' voice, the voice that kept worrying away at me with questions like 'What am I writing about?' 'Why am I writing?', meant that I produced fewer poems. Some were hopelessly dull and banal; some quite witty and clever. Between 1973 and 1975 I did an MA in the Sociology of Literature, partly because (silly old me) I thought that by doing so I would find out why I wanted to write poetry and plays. Of course I didn't find out anything of the kind, although the course was challenging and rewarding in other ways. It was also absolute agony. The pain of maintaining a careful argument, the agony of trying to write a tight, non-fiction prose that was constructed on argument and on a careful and fully conscious intellectual development is something I wrestled with, all the way through my 30,000-word dissertation. I had no room for the freedom that happens sometimes when I write poems. Everything I had to write had to be justified with instant understanding from me – that is, I couldn't splurge on to a page and then test the validity of the words from something I call a gut reaction; this is difficult to explain, because it begins to sound mystical. But that is roughly what happened. Though I wrote little poetry, and no plays during this two-and-a-half-year period, I embroidered an enormous, brightly coloured tapestry, and I did lots of knitting. That was where I found colour, not in language.

After the MA, I slowly began to turn to fiction. The return was slow. It took me a year to write one short play. I wrote a handful of poems, of which the following is, I think, an example of a poem in which the 'thought', the link with feminist critiques of culture as they were being written about in non-fiction, coheres with poetic images, and is itself, as a poem, autocritical, and 'about' poetic images. It always gets tremendous responses at poetry readings – from men and women – and I want to reproduce it as a whole because it works as a whole, and not in bits:

> *Some male poets*
>
> They write poems about
> the softness of our skin
> the curve and softness
> in our eye
> the declivity of our waist
> as we recline
>
> we are their peace, their consolation

Voices are Wild

they do not write of the rage
quivering

we snuggle perfection in
the ball of our foot
our hair weaves
glowing by lamplight
as we wait for the step
on the step

they have not written of
the power in

we approach divinity in
our life-source
we are earth-mother
yearned for
absent muse
shed a silent tear for
missed and loved

we are their comfort, their inspiration

sometimes we are regretted
when we behave
like a jealous woman
and loved for
our jealousy which
shows our devotion

they have not written of

and we have begun to
speak of it, limping
coarsely, our eyes
red with sleepless pyramids

they have written of us as
whores, devouring Liliths

and never as[8]

Apart from the fact that I think the poem coheres, and the fact that it is always a great success at readings, there is a puzzle around it. If my memory serves me right, it was somewhere about that period (second half of the 1970s) that Lacan suddenly became all the rage in some feminist theoretical circles. I have always had an odd sort of love-hate (what else?) relationship with psychoanalysis, and I got very impatient with various aspects of Lacanian theory, as well as the fact that it appeared to be the new feminist Bible. I was particularly irritated at the negativity of the idea of women's 'negative' entry into the culture. This seemed to me very different from Cora Kaplan's analysis of the taboos, since the notion of a taboo already implies both the fact of suppression and the possibility of other, alternative, oppositional kinds of creativity. In other words, it contains within it the possibility of a political dimension which gave recognition to the potential power of women in relation to the culture, whatever material position they occupy. The problem with the idea of a 'negative' entry was that the only correlation to that seemed to be that women ended up deprived of a meaningful imaginative life, of no 'positive' or creative way in which they (we) appropriated the culture. And that would mean that women had no power-base from which to begin to transform the culture. It would mean that women had no 'voice'. And you cannot build from nothing. Now of course I know that women's cultural voices are often silenced; indeed I spend a lot of my time criticising and writing about that fact. But that is not the root of the matter. Nor is it the most interesting thing. What is interesting is how, alongside the gaps and the silences, women speak and create with language the whole time. Very often we do not see ourselves what we are doing. The great and exciting thing about radical feminism was and has been and will be the way it insists that we focus on the realities of the powers we already have as women, even under capitalism or patriarchy or sexism, or whatever one terms the structures of class and sexual oppression. So the emphasis within received Lacanian thought on the 'lack' seemed to me to return to an acceptance of victimology pure and simple, of women as innocent and deprived. In other words, as 'feminine' in all the negative senses.

Now that was my conscious, argued objection to some of what I understood. And yet something prompted me to write a poem in which the silences, the absences, the lack of words at the end of some of the sections refer indirectly to an aspect of this theory. The important thing, perhaps, is that I made, invented, wove something which by its very nature proved the opposite of what it appeared to be saying. Perhaps this is what I mean when I talk about transformation, and the creation through that of a new kind of voice. In me the conscious, political voice was combating a theory; the subconscious poetical voice was recognising the validity of some of the theory; out of the contradiction between these two came the speech and voice that is the poem. That is how I see it now.

I want, finally, to look at voice and language in yet another way, and to link that back to recent forms of fictional voice with which I have been working, and which feel to me like some kind of breakthrough, some kind of possible solution to what I have lived with through the 1970s: the apparent conflict between the rationality of theory and political writing, and the wildness, the relative unpredictability of a poem, and sometimes a play. I think I can date the change from about 1981, but I imagine that things must have been stirring before that. But in 1981 one thing is sure: my mother died. Something about that trauma, something I don't fully understand yet, has begun a process that is – as far as poetry is concerned – taking me, drawing me back to certain roots which I have ignored or thought unimportant.

First of all, I am Jewish. Well. There's a story. Or many stories. Anyway. Then, my parents were Polish/Russian immigrants, at the beginning of the century. I was born here. My parents spoke English, Yiddish and Hebrew, and my mother also spoke German and Polish. The language I learned to speak was English, but I must have been absorbing quite a lot of the Yiddish even then. English is the basic language in which I communicate, it is the language I was educated in, and the language in which I read and write. But at different times in my life I have spoken and thought in both German and Hebrew, and I worked with French as part of my university degree. I am not really as multi-lingual as all that sounds; the point is that although English has always been my chief language, at different times I have been dislocated from it, and also freed from it into other kinds of possibility for language; the elegance of French; the brick-building structure of German; the distance between Biblical Hebrew and modern, idiomatic Hebrew; the 'homeliness' of Yiddish. The latter was brought home to me recently when there was a reshowing of a 1930s version of the Yiddish film 'The Dybbuk'. It was the first Yiddish film I had seen, and it was the first time I had heard Yiddish spoken outside Jewish homes. In my mind Yiddish was associated with families, with domestic things, with food, eating, rows, with all the contradictions of family intimacy. And here was this language being used for a drama, for a work of art. I began to realise how 'personal' to me Yiddish felt, and that was a strange discovery to make after so many years.

Being Jewish in British literary culture (political or not) is no bean feast. America is quite different. The rhythms of Yiddish, the 'Jewish' sense of humour, the weight of Jewish suffering, has become far more integral to the development of American literature in general than it has ever been here. The reasons are material and obvious; but it means that to have a sense of one's self as a British Jewish writer, is already to state a dislocation, to face basic questions about how you use the English language, what rhythms do you pick up on, how do you challenge the perfection of the middle-class, or even upper-class, social-realist sentence. I had enough trouble being a woman and a feminist, now I have to discover I am Jewish.

To return to 1981. Sometime during the year I decided it was time I read the Old Testament. That's how I thought of it. Of course – silly me – I should have realised that what I was actually embarking on was a re-reading of the Old Testament. The familiarity of it kept surprising me. I was reading it in English, but the Biblical rhythms in English set off a whole lot of Hebrew rhythms; so many phrases and sections were familiar, in the sense that I knew them without ever having made the effort to learn them by heart. Bits of the stories were familiar to me. As I read through, a bit every night, I began having very powerful reactions; the buzz of recognition, an admiration for the beauty of the lyricism, absolute fury at the theology. I began answering back, eccentrically, as I felt, when I felt, and found I was doing so in two kinds of 'voice'. Over the next year or two these voices crystallised as Eve and Lilith. About Eve I don't have to say much. But Lilith – for anyone who doesn't know, in secular Jewish myth Lilith was Adam's first wife, who transgressed by refusing to adopt the missionary position, and who also transgressed by 'naming' the Lord. For this she was banished to limbo, and Eve was made in her place.

The two voices became the basis for the longest and most

concerted poetic work I have yet written. It is 'me' in a number of senses which I can only begin to pin down. There is the Jewishness of the source material. There is Eve the mother, who has to find her own identity. There is Lilith, angry, questioning, fighting, working for art as well as identity. And they are poems with ironies that come from me and Yiddish, with imagery which makes sense to me. I began publicly reading some of the poems while I was writing them, and they get tremendous responses from audiences, whatever their hue. There feels at the moment to be a way in which three 'margin' voices, voices from exile, Jewish, woman and feminist, can make sense in relation to a dominant voice. After all, the language and rhythms of the Old Testament have influenced the development of English Literature, its rhythms, its moralism, its toughness, its self-confidence. Of course the voices of classical Eng. Lit. come also from its imperial dominance, from its male-gendered bias as well; but I suppose for me a rather gleeful irony has emerged: good old England, with its lousy record of anti-Semitism until about the past hundred years, when things have got better for Jews, this good old England, like the whole of the Christian religion, is built upon the Jewishness of the Old Testament. This is probably the most obvious fact in the world to everyone reading this, but my point here is that as far as I am concerned, there has been some kind of mechanism which has made me hide this from myself, and now it is beginning to reach the 'thinking' me, as opposed to the me who could not come to terms with the fact, could not transform the fact into my own voice. The me who tried to separate my Jewishness from my other literary voices, and who has decided that isn't on all the time any more. And of course, the irony of middle- and upper-class English writing has always been one of the things that endeared me so much to it, which, in its own way, made me very receptive to the very open and jagged forms which I quoted at the beginning of this. Along with the idiomatic and syllabic rhythms of medieval Spanish Jewish poetry which inform my own open-ish forms, even in the Eve and Lilith sequence, which I have mentioned already.

Recently, I've begun to delve back into the history of Jewish cultures, in part to rediscover my own 'roots', but also to try and make some kind of literary sense of the relationship between the me that is part of the non-Englishness of being Jewish, and the me that is part of the central canon of classical English literature. And in the course of this eclectic delving, I am pondering over the great irony that the period of the flowering of early English literature, the Middle Ages through the Renaissance to the Elizabethan period, was one in which Jews were pretty well absent from England. Jews were banished in the thirteenth century; and the importance of the English Bible, and its Jewishness, and its influence on secular literature, was conducted in the absence of the people to whom the Old Testament belonged.

A fascinating example of cultural appropriation, and one which has great bearing on the simultaneous marginality and centrality of my own voice, or voices. I refuse to be bound by any one literary tone, just as I refuse to be bound by any one literary genre. Or I refuse to be bound because I don't feel that one genre does everything I want. And so my voices are wide and wild and sometimes varied. And in the real world this makes it hard for me to be categorised by publishers, critics, readers. It means I feel the continuous pressure to shout, continual uncertainty that my voice may not be heard, because it does not run smoothly into any single, clear channel. Perhaps this too is the source of the density I quoted at the beginning, perhaps this is the source of my dissatisfaction with a merely satirical/polemic tone.

I can't tell where my current excavation will lead. But one place it has also led - this direct tone, that feels directly part of me - is to a clarifying of my non-fiction prose style. I no longer feel I have to imitate serious academic writers (feminist or other); or write in theoretical/scientific formulations; I feel I can begin to play with non-fiction in a more eclectic way, and return in fiction, but with a different voice, to my earlier poetic style.

And since I cautioned you at the beginning to take the accounts of a writer as evidence and illumination, and not as a definitive guide, I want to finish with two of the poems from the Eve and Lilith sequence. They come from a book called *Gardens of Eden*[9] which was turned down by a number of publishers, straight, socialist and feminist, first because they said 'poetry doesn't sell' (rubbish, if you do it right) and second (and this is my hypothesis) because it was Jewish and like nothing they had read. In one case a small alternative publisher returned the manuscript with a long list of scholarly sources on Lilith which he thought I ought to read. Forget it. Here is the art, here is the poetry. These are only two out of sixty poems. The others need to be read too.

Lilith, in the Morning

abstract art must truly be divine
for did not the Lord say

'thou shalt not make unto
thee any graven images or any likeness
of any thing that is in heaven above
or that is in the earth beneath
or that is in the water under the earth'   Exodus 20:4

gold and silver and brass

blue   purple   scarlet   linen
goat's hair

        oil for light   spices for anointing   oil
incense   onyx
                        emerald   sapphire
diamond   agate   amethyst
blue lace
                        bread and lamb

my burnt offerings
my tabernacle, my temple: art

myrrh   cinammon
olive oil

frankincense
                        stone tablets
pillars of cloud and fire

shining faces
almonds   flowers

oh God

Eve, in the Morning

So God created man (sic) in his (sic) own image?

'Male and female he created them'   Genesis 1:27

Look
it was only a tree, for God's sake
a nice tree
nice shade, green, leaves
an apple

You eat one apple and they remember you forever; you
only want to be left in peace, make
chutney, compote, dried apple rings
on a string

a snake? don't be silly
knowledge? you read too many Good Books
naked? so I like the sun. I tan easy.

Hava. Eve. Me

Sarah, Abraham's wife, the mother of Israel?
Well, let me tell you
you
couldn't tell
my chicken soup
from hers

you work your ribs to the bone
setting up the human race
and do you get any thanks?
a *nächtige tug* you get thanks
for freezing in
a goddam garden

I was glad we had to move, get
a decent place
those ants everywhere
and I mean everywhere

well, I've got a lot of grandchildren now

a little too much begetting, maybe
but as long as they've got their health and strength

I was always a good mother
no-one can say I wasn't
a good mother.

Please explore the others.

Notes

1. *Aurora Leigh and Other Poems*, intro. Cora Kaplan (The Women's Press, London, 1978), p. 9.
2. Ibid., p. 10.
3. Michelene Wandor, *Understudies: Theatre and Sexual Politics*, (Methuen, London, 1981); Michelene Wandor (ed.), *Plays by Women*, 3 vols (Methuen, London, 1982–84).
4. Michelene Wandor with Michèle Roberts and Judith Kazantzis, *Touch Papers* (Allison & Busby, London, 1982), p. 80.
5. Michelene Wandor, *Upbeat, Poems and Stories* (Journeyman Press, London, 1982), p. 39.
6. Ibid.
7. Ibid., p. 36.
8. Ibid., p. 44.
9. Michelene Wandor, *Gardens of Eden: Poems for Eve and Lilith* (Journeyman/Playbooks, London, 1984).

5

FEMINIST LITERARY CRITICISM IN AMERICA AND ENGLAND

Maggie Humm

Nationalism is to feminists what humanism is to Marxists: that which must be cast out. To answer the question, 'what is feminist criticism?' then, it would seem obvious to say that it is the analysis of a universal sexual representation and ideology in literature from the point of view of women. But there is a curious way in which feminist criticism in America or England is more recognisably like other American or English criticism (written by men) than it is universally feminist. The various operations that feminist critics carry on have distinct national character-istics. Most American criticism, concentrated within academia, takes literature to have a gendered set of meanings as signifying practices. Most English criticism claims to be about culture in a broader political sense and therefore often *collectively* examines literary genres in order to situate signifying practices ethno-graphically in women's everyday lives.

Clearly, feminist literary criticism has no *single hegemonic* national ideology either in America or England. Neither is it possible to document the whole proliferation of literary crit-icism in both countries. There are helpful subject bibliographies which cover writers and criticism (Evans, 1979). But a national comparison can help us re-evaluate what relationship literary criticism *can* make between women's writing, social relations and lived experience. The challenge as I see it, is by fully understanding each other's criticism to counter more adequately patriarchal traditions with a unified feminist criticism, since it would appear that otherwise American feminists will stay closer to American patterns and English feminists to English critical traditions than to each other.

Of course feminist criticism as part of the organic relation between feminist teachers and the women's movement in both countries does provide one significant contrast to the male tradition honestly characterised by Raymond Williams as 'commodity' criticism (Williams, 1976). Working *first* as archaeology and *then* as theory feminist criticism is a major departure from the male, or particularly Marxist, tradition. Feminist literary criticism in America and England starts from the same base. Feminists in both countries share a need for a place and a stance from which to ask reparations from patriarchal precedents. American and British women's studies has done much to change the androcentric bias of literary studies. In both countries it has brought to attention previously neglected and undervalued women writers, and thereby changed the concept of writing as an activity. Women as critics however have received much less attention here or there, and therefore the ground plan of literary *criticism* has not changed direction from dominant patriarchal theory as radically as has the literary *canon*. But it would be sad if British women critics' often very precise codification of feminist as opposed to female concerns forced them to a judgemental position on American writing for its less overtly political perspective. In the main, influential feminist texts in Britain have always come from outside, from Simone de Beauvoir's *The Second Sex* to Kate Millett's *Sexual Politics* or Adrienne Rich's *Of Woman Born*. But an English Left obsession with 'realism' and 'anti-humanism' subsequently demands that writing reveals social as much as critical relationships and is therefore frequently antipathetic to American 'experimental' needs. As in the hostile reception of American writings on bisexuality (Buck, 1983). Rather, feminist literary criticism will need to weld American with English concerns and techniques in order to escape from the stranglehold of national tradition.

How then do feminists define the act of literary criticism in America and in England and how can we benefit from our distinctive interpretations, methods and strategies? First our critical traditions, institutions and topics are dissimilar. Second, in very general terms, American criticism links definitions of women's difference with syntactics rather than, as in England, with precise political positions and groups. This makes our relationship to feminist theory, and use of other disciplines, in particular psychoanalysis, divergent. Finally, although both America and England do share a reader-centred perspective, Americans have valorised women's difference while the English, in the work of the Birmingham Centre for Cultural Studies, *Screen* and *Feminist Review*, have detailed women's cultural *oppression* in collective readings. What are the reasons for this divergence? Perhaps the greater influence of feminist art criticism has focused American approaches on female iconography (Lippard, 1976; Chicago, 1979). Perhaps there is a general American need for belief in a wild zone. Fetterley called her book 'a self-defense survival manual for a reader lost in the masculine wilderness of the American novel' (Fetterley, 1978). A different disciplinary influence, mainly from left-wing history groups such as Ruskin History Workshop and writers like Sheila Rowbotham, has led to an English socialist stress on *opposition* rather than *expression*.

This national political difference is reflected in the two countries' different modes of writing. The gaining of an intellectual territory has led many American feminists to stress the primacy of traditional intellectual skills. Skills giving access to intellectual life can often create a strong suspicion of approaches which seem to undermine the importance of content. Criticising literature in this sense is about developing a capacity for feelings about new and varied content (whether black, lesbian or androgynous). Social relations, when discussed, are selected for their ability to count as experience and methods are a search for instruments, like the oral diary, which can locate feelings (Fisher, 1979). The American feminist critic has found Shakespeare's sister.

The whole direction of English feminist literary criticism – as Ros Coward's key question 'Are women's novels feminist novels?' suggests that concentrating on female experience *per se* need not at all be a feminist gesture (Coward, 1980). For English feminists, feminist literary criticism needs a precise notion of a *shared* female culture contesting traditional meanings. English arguments are often not about the nature of literature but about political decisions of what makes a work feminist and on what grounds (Montefiore, 1983). Criticism here plays a mediating role between the literary text and social history, in a thematic concern with the representation of domesticity or patriarchy.

The 'Different' Traditions

Both English and American critics share the same goal – to provide women with a women's world. They have done this by re-examining published women writers usually with a thematic approach and finding common motifs and feminine images. They have delineated important characters in women's writing as role models of enlightened heroines. They have found and revalidated lost and ignored women writers and, by mixing lost women with those already secured, criticism has created an alternative great female tradition (Showalter, 1979). By utilising material from psychology, anthropology and art history in particular, American feminist criticism finds alternative patterns of signification within women's writing – from gift-giving to dance metaphors.

English feminists seem to start from a different tradition – one of prescriptive criticism, a method developed by Marxist critics which evaluates literature according to its alignment with specific ideological premises, adopted by some feminists in an attempt to subvert the patriarchal presuppositions incorporated in literature.

It would be too simple to suggest that Americans read their culture 'psychoanalytically' for its specificity and English critics read their culture 'politically' for its positions. But since feminist criticism assumes that literature describes the distinctive patterns of life of women and gives them expressive form then feminists in each country will inevitably use distinctive critical methods and explanations in terms of their social and material experience.

One of the first and most influential American critics was Mary Ellman in *Thinking About Women* (Ellman, 1968). Ellman reads culture as literary history. For example, she suggests, as servants became less available in Edwardian society they took

93

Women's Writing

on a more disciplinary function in fiction as in *Lady Chatterley's Lover*. Female stereotypes, Ellman considers, are created at a time of social unrest. It is the codification of experience by women writers into doubles and opposites which has enabled them, Ellman suggests, to avoid male pomposity. But simply by charting the consistency of stereotypes as a literary phenomenon Ellman assumes society itself to be a unified group of phenomena defined in opposition to the Other of Woman.

Ellen Moers' *Literary Women* became the classic example of this approach (Moers, 1977). *Literary Women* translates aspects of female culture into the problematic relation between female experience and forms in female writing. Moers claims that there are specific female genres (the Gothic), myths (birth imagery in *Frankenstein*) and specific female symbols (like Anne Frank's bird). Women's social resistance becomes, for Moers, a matter of style – the no-saying of Jane Eyre is an attack by Charlotte Brontë on the cultural conditioning of young girls.

Literary Women did open up a new way of thinking about the literary inheritance of women writers. Harold Bloom characterised male writers in *The Anxiety of Influence* as fighters *against* their literary forefathers (Bloom, 1979). Ellen Moers, on the other hand, describes the warmth and regard of women writers for each other like George Eliot and Harriet Beecher Stowe or Emily Dickinson's debt to Elizabeth Barrett Browning. But Moers sees literary form in very functional ways and mainly for its function in the characterisation of white, heterosexual heroines. The drawback to Moers' project is both her very unproblematic assumption of a writer's intention and her homophobia (Gardiner, 1982).

Sandra M. Gilbert and Susan Gubar's *The Madwoman in the Attic* shows the utility of Moers' model (Gilbert and Gubar, 1979). They describe the works of Jane Austen, Mary Shelley, the Brontës and George Eliot among others and claim that it is in images (of enclosure, of doubles, of disease and landscape) that women writers strategically redefine themselves, art and society.

The book throws out a number of interesting ideas – that women writers are closest to characters they detest, that their images are anxieties about their own creativity. But the form of *The Madwoman in the Attic* is revealing. Its 718 pages show how

94

much Gilbert and Gubar have depended on narrative, on paraphrase, rather than precise analysis. They go from writer to writer with no concluding chapter. They cannot conclude because they have constructed no argument. It is a curiously static text which gives little sense of why we *would* read one writer more than another.

The book's narrative, rather than analytic form is due, as Gilbert and Gubar themselves admit, to its derivation from a course they taught at Indiana University and thus is emblematic of the situation of feminist criticism in American institutions. Similarly Patricia Meyer Spacks' *The Female Imagination*, which is also a thematic study, is organised around teachable titles which can encompass a variety of otherwise disparate works (Spacks, 1977). Her titles of 'power' and 'passivity' resemble Gilbert and Gubar's 'angel' and clearly enabled them, as teachers, to swap around texts from year to year.

Female stereotypes in women's literature are its most accessible feature but motifs are equally accessible themes in much else of western literature. Not only are they vague but they lock the disparate qualities of any text into crude polarities. While there may be a general tendency in women's writing to oppositional values, charting it uncontextualised does not explain why one stereotype is more useful than any other. The problem here, as with Elizabeth Hardwick's *Seduction and Betrayal* (Hardwick, 1974) or Susan Koppleman Cornillon's *Images of Women in Fiction: Feminist Perspectives* (Cornillon, 1972), is a restriction to character as solution to culture. More important are the metaphysical implications of the 'female heroine' approach. By conceptualising the female heroine as an integral subject coincident with her own consciousness critics suggest a unitary subject – the female. The implication is that women could be free agents. English feminists would challenge the metaphysical fiction that women could be free agents in a women's world. Annette Kuhn's argument in her film studies, for example, is that the representation of women is part of the moment of *reception* as much as the moment of production (Kuhn, 1982). The American 'female heroine' critic has avoided the way literary texts are aggregates of social institutions, forms of linguistic organisation, practices and subjects which cannot answer a single casual explanation.

Later American feminists have used Lacan and Derrida to enlarge concepts of the literary text as a locus of cultural relations impossible to totalise. Judith Kegan Gardiner and Gayatri Spivak speak most of the influence of French theory on their conceptions of feminist culture. For Gardiner the key terms are power, desire and difference and she attacks the male critic Frederick Jameson precisely because he defined history as that which refuses desire (Gardiner, 1982). She understands that much critical theory, as with Barbara Johnson's work, is like psychoanalytic object relations theory in identifying the female with the Other. That is, with a long list of everything that is not the male self, including nature, mothers or the absent. Gardiner is careful to stress that although it is useful for us to understand some of the negative ways we are apprehended in dominant culture, it is important for us ourselves not to equate and confuse these categories and collapse them into one single category of difference.

More than most feminists Adrienne Rich has described the cultural and literary expectations of her readers (women students) and the way she, and other writers, have responded to these expectations. In *On Lies, Secrets, and Silence* she describes criticism institutionally as well as an individual process (Rich, 1980). Ritual, to Adrienne Rich, is what realises, or objectivates, for women a meaningful life. Ritual is a linguistic map of meaning which stands for a pattern of social organisation. Adrienne Rich's influential essay, 'Jane Eyre: The Temptations of a Motherless Woman', takes *Jane Eyre* to be a ritual of women's social and cultural reflexes against the male Victorian world (Rich, 1980), In *Of Woman Born* Rich took motherhood *out* of the ghetto of reflexive culture by situating its rituals in a longer historical view (Rich, 1977). Rich carved a new history for mothers in myth and ritual in a very exciting model of female cultural power.

Of Woman Born is an original form of feminist criticism in its mix of anthropology, literature and autobiography. It has not been succeeded by any criticism in as ambitious or hybrid a form. The problem with Rich's position is perhaps due to a problem in feminism itself – its desire for a confirmed past. Like many feminists Rich takes rituals to be a *response* to environment. While women's rituals are, or can be, sites of struggle against the hegemony of male power we must distinguish between ritual *activities* in literature and the historical terms and ideology within which they take place. But as Kristéva has argued, the symbolic contract has been women's sacrificial social contract (Kristéva, 1981).

It is in her own 'cultural' form that Adrienne Rich is most successful as a critic. In her autobiographical critical essays she crosses self and other to blur public and private. She aims to tell women readers how to read women writers; and how women readers can tell women writers how to write.

Rich's major contribution has been to mine the terrain of feminist criticism for the wealth of lesbian and black culture (Rich, 1983). Her crucial essay, 'Compulsory Heterosexuality and Lesbian Existence', has generated much debate (Kaplan, 1983). But by greatly enlarging the categories of lesbianism and black culture, and hence revising their system of representation Rich sets up contradictions and distinctions which can counter patriarchal ideology.

Lesbian feminist criticism arose directly through the political activities of the lesbian community and the feminist movement in America. Never easily integrated into academic institutions, it has provided American feminist criticism in the 1980s with a new dimension. A. Snitow's essay in *Desire* is a very good introduction to these major shifts in American feminism which occurred through debates about sexuality and culture (Snitow *et al.*, 1984).

American feminist criticism in the 1970s is best summed up in the writings of four critics – Ellen Moers, Patricia Meyer Spacks, Elaine Showalter and Florence Howe. In their work they began to develop a female annex to male literature. This led them to redefinitions of the topic of criticism because recognition of a new group of works turns out to be more than a simple process of addition and at some point feminists needed new critical tools. The new grouping or configuration tended to alter our definitions and hierarchies and our understanding of how those definitions and hierarchies came into being.

The two key essays of Elaine Showalter illustrate most clearly this major work of American feminist criticism. In 'Towards a Feminist Poetics' she divides criticism into two distinct varieties. For Showalter the first type is concerned with woman as reader,

97

as the consumer of male-produced literature, and with the way in which the hypothesis of a female reader changes our view of a text. The second type of feminist critic is concerned with woman as writer – with woman as the producer of textual meaning, with the history, themes, genres and structures of literature by women. Here she theorises the more empirical revisionism of her earlier book *A Literature of Their Own* (Showalter, 1978). Showalter went on to develop her ideas in 'Feminist Criticism in the Wilderness' and subsequent writings (Showalter, 1982). This categorises what might be called working techniques of criticism in her discussion of biological, linguistic and psychological models of 'different' discourse.

Other American feminist critics have taken their position from reactions to, and attacks on, Showalter's writings. Showalter's failure adequately to address issues of race and sexuality, to these later feminists, is symptomatic of the inadequacies of white, heterosexual women's studies in American universities. Carolyn J. Allen set out a role for criticism as a political act in her response to Showalter's essay (Allen, 1982). Bulkin, more than others, has attacked the homophobia and racism of these earlier women and those critics most influenced by them like Annette Kolodny (Kolodny, 1980). American shifts seem often breathtakingly contemporary to outsiders, but it is in the work of Adrienne Rich, Lilian Faderman, Gayatri Spivak and Elly Bulkin that a new focus for American feminism does receive serious attention.

For Bulkin women speak to women across periods but within distinct categories of race or sexual preference. The quest for a lineage is now much less a quest for women's history *per se* and more a tracing of themes *within* black lesbian writing or *within* white lesbian writers, as with the work on Alice Walker's debt to Zora Neale Hurston (Hull, 1977).

Bulkin's concern has, to an English eye, a very American as opposed to generally feminist, position. Her search is for groups of outsiders in American society who lack a stake in American social/political or aesthetic values as determined by white, middle-class American men or women (Bulkin, 1980). Each group is identified as one who reacts against the literary tradition and has sought to establish an anti-literary/anti-intellectual history of their own. When delineating those 'histories' however, critics like Bulkin define opposition often in aesthetic rather than political terms. Each minority group seems to use the same investigative techniques, the same parallel features or rituals, symbols, forms and purposes. In her book collections *Lesbian Fiction* (Bulkin, 1981) and *Lesbian Poetry* (Bulkin, 1981) she draws a history of opposition which relies, not on traditions of social class, but of linguistic type in the debts Bulkin spells out for her coteries to American oral traditions of the Bible, Native Americans and the Beats.

For English feminist critics the text alone cannot provide *the* signifying opposition. In the work of the Birmingham Centre for Cultural Studies (McRobbie, 1981), the texts of Michèle Barrett (Barrett, 1982) and Patricia Stubbs (Stubbs, 1981), English critics tend to look for themes of family, of public or private spaces, rather than fantasy or difference.

The criticism generated by the women's liberation movement in Britain came very much out of the immediate situation in the 1960s and 1970s. Left-wing politics, the peace movement and radical psychiatry were strands used in many writings to oppose conservative notions of society and culture. On the one hand women critics often used cultural writers, such as Althusser, rather than literary critics to reach an understanding of how literary traditions and educational institutions oppress women (Belsey, 1982). On the other a body of work emerged from Marxist–feminism concentrating on the ideological construction of women's exploitation by the media (Baehr, 1981).

Feminism for Girls provides a good example of this second approach (McRobbie, 1981). Angela McRobbie and others use a narrative approach detailing kinds of discrimination experienced by adolescent girls as constructed in the literary and visual style of the magazines they read. Feminist criticism here is about the reception and subversion of imagery. The approach can be characterised as a semiotic analysis of depictions of reality, or unreality, as modes of signification both for their audience and us as readers. Criticism then has become an ethnographic, rather than literary, setting-up of questions about culture and the creation of alternatives.

Treating a socially situated reader as a discursive construct in the text has also been one of the methods of English feminist work on soap operas and film. This trajectory starts from the desire to examine genres which are popular with contemporary women. The objective of much of this criticism has been to address the paradox that women's popular culture speaks to women's pleasure at the same time that it puts it into the service of the patriarchal family (Williamson, 1978).

Although feminist work, in England, on the genre of romantic fiction has enlarged the boundaries of what we can call 'literature' there are weaknesses in the approach as an *explanation* of literary patterning. By describing ethnographically the role of literary culture within women's experience, this criticism has often refused any framework of 'good' or 'bad' representation aesthetically. Meaning then can only be the result of a changing interaction between particular verbal forms and socially constructed readers. While the notion of meaning, in this sense, as an ideological force is often very well demonstrated, it ignores the whole issue of literary value. The refusal of aesthetic values is also evident in an English preference for juxtaposition in collections of disciplinary approaches like *The Rights and Wrongs of Women* rather than theorising within the discipline of literary studies as such (Mitchell and Oakley, 1976). Rather than taking the literary text as artefact *within* criticism English feminists prefer to work from collective groups whose aim is agenda-setting rather than the more purist lexicographical role of American criticism (Marxist–Feminist Literature Collective, 1978).

Feminist/Marxist criticism in England has stayed with the notion that the politics of a text are a function of its context as much as of its style or form. Writers like Terry Lovell treat aesthetics almost as a political strategy (Lovell, 1983). English psychoanalytic critics such as Ros Coward also prefer to see the act of criticism as the uncovering of cultural ideologies. Her continuing project is to understand textual representations as part of the cultural institutions which produce and circulate those representations (Coward, 1982).

English critics then see meaning not in the formulation of *literary* experience but in deciding what can be saved from the terrain of 'literature' for feminist politics.

Michèle Barrett has done most to link theories of historical materialism with definitions of women in literature. She provides crucial insights into the relation in particular between the class position of Virginia Woolf and Woolf's system of literary values (Barrett, 1979). It is this insight into Woolf which is my reason for choosing Barrett as the critic to represent English feminist Marxists since I can make a direct comparison between her position on Woolf and that of the feminist Marxist (who works in America) Gayatri Spivak's view of Woolf's *To the Lighthouse* (Spivak, 1980). The comparison will make clear the different cultural concerns of English and American feminists.

Reading Barrett and Spivak is like reading accounts not only of two very different critics but as if they were writing about two very different authors. Barrett starts from the question 'What are the consequences for the woman author of historical changes in the position of women in society?', and her text is then an analysis of the historical determinants of Woolf's literary/critical production. Barrett gives a very good account of the relation between Virginia Woolf's lack of formal education, her critical reception (or lack of it) by male critics, her domestic isolation and the inevitable effect of these forces on her work. Woolf's writings on sexuality, therefore, are seen mainly in relation to Woolf's other positions on male belligerence and fascism and the relationship of bourgeois sexual morality to Victorian society. Barrett shies away from Woolf's commitment to female difference preferring to see Woolf's argument for difference as social rather than biologically constructed. Sexuality and its multiple forms are precisely Spivak's very 'different' point of departure. Her critique is like much recent American criticism heavily in debt to Lacan and Derrida (whom Spivak has translated and introduced to American audiences). Spivak's text also illustrates the debt American feminists owe to their disciplinary training in rhetoric and linguistics as undergraduates. Woolf is now translated into allegory and verbal dexterity – a move away from representation and the social creation of art. Spivak attempts to understand *To the Lighthouse* by reading it as the deliberate superimposition of two allegories – the grammatical and the sexual. These are present, Spivak claims, in Woolf's two languages – the language of art and the language of marriage. By an extended pun on the word copula, both as a pivot of grammar and as a sexual activity, Spivak makes a Derrida-like business of the different uses and meanings of single words. Hers

101

is not a continuous textual analysis (there is none of Barrett's thorough cultural history) but rather a use of what Raymond Williams would call key words which can represent key grammatical and cultural moments.

The difference between English and American feminism could not be clearer. English criticism is shown to be illustrative in its welding of social and literary concerns. American criticism is shown to be formalist and assuming an agreed notion of the avant-garde. Both critics offer helpful ways of reading Woolf. By taking a more overtly sexual text like *Orlando* we could (*a la* Barrett) see Orlando's development and gender changes in relation to the literary and historical styles she/he encounters. The critical focus here would be Orlando's attack on Victorian culture and masculinity. Conversely (*a la* Spivak), we could look at *Orlando* as a deliberately uncommitted narrative whose biographer 'slips away' textually to show the difficulty of transsexuality. Since gender difference is *only* described physiologically by Woolf, this reading reveals the sub-text of physcial violence as displayed in Orlando's mixture of interrogative and interior analysis.

I would call both feminist readings and have applied the English and American approaches simply as a personal example of how the two models can balance, rather than prescriptively cancel each other out. Of course there are Marxist/American feminists who also chart the sociology of women's literary culture (Fox-Genovese, 1980). But the marker that distinguishes English and American interpretations of literature is their alternative notions of the 'difference' of women's culture.

Difference and Theory

Hypotheses about the origins and perpetuation of differentiation, of the feminine and masculine, do not lie only in the province of literary criticism. Some American feminist critics acknowledge that sources crucial to their feminism are not located in traditional critical methodologies and have turned to psychoanalysis and its uses in French theory (Gallop, 1982). But in reviewing American and English notions of 'difference' in *literary* criticism we can understand the problematic relation between feminist literary criticism and feminist ideology. This helps deal with the complex issue of how various forms of literary criticism relate more to ideological and institutional than literary critical positions.

Stephen Heath defines a masculine discourse as one 'which fails to take account of the problem of sexual difference in its enunciation and address' (Heath, 1978). And at best difference is usually defined in its epistemological aspects – women think in circles rather than lines, we tend to be holistic rather than partial; we prefer open to closed systems; we employ associational rather than sequential logic; we are obsessed with detail and with pattern; that we write sentences to quote Virginia Woolf 'of a more elastic fibre than the old'; that we are subjective and naturally attracted to interior spaces, children and animals.

This is to deal with difference without constituting an *opposition*, and the stance is perhaps more appropriate to earlier American critics. Earlier critics like Grace Stewart look at difference more in terms of polarisation which is a theatrical representation of difference. Her critical technique is an etymological categorising of women's qualities (Stewart, 1978). Later critics like the writers represented in Elizabeth Abel's collection *Writing and Sexual Difference* or Alice Jardine's *The Future of Difference* are dealing with the more Lacanian instability of difference. The critical technique here is to document *l'écriture féminine* in an overt connection between language and revolution (Abel, 1982).

Other American critics who look for the essentially 'feminine' are Patricia Spacks and Ellen Moers. But Nina Auerbach's *Community of Women* is the classic example of this approach. Auerbach describes corporate visions of women's groups in the work of Brontë, Gaskell and Spark among others (Auerbach, 1978). She is interested in the way women's communities create a 'difference' from those of men, particularly in the way women replace male explicit and inspirational codes of behaviour with codes that are whispered and in buried language. Difference then is defined emblematically with communities of women as emblems of female self-sufficiency. Auerbach has that wonderful American faith in a new frontier. For her, communities of women have a miraculous ability to create themselves and offer an attractive idea of power in their networks of social or professional concerns (as in her analysis of Mrs Gaskell's *Cranford*). But the problem here is Auerbach's restriction of difference to the idea of female heroines and thus ultimately female stereotypes.

The first American adequately to promote 'difference' was Adrienne Rich. As Kristéva, Rich rethinks the maternal domain to create a new language of criticism. Altogether the dialogue between psychoanalysis and literature has been invaluable for a feminist rethinking of textual power (Gallop, 1982). The reading techniques of Irigaray are particularly influential in American criticism. Irigaray does not offer a definitive reading of a text, closing it or making it her property but only notes those phrases which seem interpretable so as to induce her reader to complete both critical and primary texts. An American feminist reader of Irigaray – Shoshana Felman – has gone further to suggest that 'literature in psychoanalysis is its unthought' and literature therefore represents psychoanalysis's condition of possibility (Hartman, 1978). The point here is to read symbolisation in literature (as French psychoanalysis does) as an instrument of growth not repression. Psychoanalysis has been important to American critics because it makes the debate about subjectivity and difference central to feminism, and because it enlarges any account of the possibilities of femininity. It also, congenially, provides Americans with a new frontier, a wild zone of bisexuality and the imaginary.

A concern with wilderness and wild metaphors can be found in almost all the articles in Elizabeth Abel's *Writing and Sexual Difference*. Elaine Showalter's essay discussed earlier is called 'Feminist Criticism in the Wilderness'; Susan Gubar deals with the emblematic representation of women's forbidden blood in Isak Dinesen; Annette Kolodny uses captivity narratives of the frontier west; Catherine Stimpson discusses the fluidity and 'wildness' of gender structures in her consideration of lesbian writing; Nancy J. Vickers reviews the Petrarchan tradition of fragmentary descriptions of the female body; and Gayatri Spivak presents a text/translation of the Bengali Devi's acount of women's transgression, exclusion and mutilation (Abel, 1982).

In art for a long time men have fragmented, distorted and cut women's bodies into pieces of false perspective. Now American feminist critics are using techniques of narcissism and anatomical exaggeration positively to evade patriarchal categorisation. Where English critics prefer to see gender difference historically as constituted in diverse sets of ideological practices as in the work of Ros Coward, American feminists have been extending the frontiers of critical practice in their innovative uses of associations and metaphors.

At its best finding a China has challenged the supposed objectivity of literary standards by re-defining 'experience' and 'discourse' through its examination of hitherto repressed femininity. Alice Ostriker's 'Body Language' (Ostriker, 1980) is a good example of the way we *can* read women poets (she assesses Plath, Sexton and Rich) in terms of their shared refusal of male cursive distance and women's 'different' relation to the symbolic as a version of the social contract.

Again the frontier wilderness, the journey to it, and stories about it by settler women, has been emblematic of other women's alternative writing and psychic possibilities (Mason and Green, 1979).

The collection of English critical essays which comes closest to the American construction of difference is one made by Mary Jacobus in *Women Writing and Writing About Women* (perhaps because Jacobus is herself American). Jacobus and other contributors start from the position (denigrated by Ros Coward) that there is a self-defining tradition of women's writing (Jacobus, 1979). The critical focus here is on each text's subversion of the 'censorship' inherent in any patriarchal agenda-setting within literary genres – whether of realism or romanticism. The critical objective is to assess syntactical patterns of slippage or dislocation as representative of women's shared refusal of aspects of language itself.

The collection is mortgaged to conventional criticism in its over-concentration on nineteenth-century novels, but its preoccupation with syntax is radical in its implications. The 'materiality' of each text, they claim, can be found in its detailed syntactical processes.

But neither in these contributions, nor in American notions of difference, do we discover why language *has* to foreground political conditions. There is a revealing coda in Jacobus's own account of *Villette* where she explains that she is reading *Villette* as a double text because she herself faces that other disjunction between academic and private experience.

This mode of criticism does not escape the fallacy of defining the feminine entirely by its 'Otherness', but has however answered the question of whether in reading we *must* apply a gender consciousness to that reading by a resounding YES.

Reader Approaches

Reader-response criticism has been the most significant contemporary development in both American and English feminist literary criticism. It is not a conceptually unified critical position (as it is not in male critics using it who have also presented a variety of orientations).

I would like to compare the most representative reader-response criticism in each country assessing the Americans Judith Fetterley, Kate Millett and the pioneering Louise Rosenblatt, and in England the texts of the Birmingham Centre for Cultural Studies, because I believe the approach has altered the whole terrain of criticism, and also that its impact does point up and finally focus national distinctions and characteristics. But first, I shall briefly review the themes of reader-response criticism in order to introduce the field and assess the much longer tradition of male criticism to draw lessons for feminist critics.

Reader-response criticism is part of disciplinary moves within literary criticism toward self-reflexiveness because it questions and makes explicit the assumptions that ground the methods of literary criticism and concurrently the critic's role in creating literature as an object of study.

In America the approach has helped feminists in the deconstruction of American literary figures like Hemingway and Mailer, and in England it has helped to spread an idea of collective reading in women's groups. The objectivity of the literary text is the concept which this criticism eventually destroys. And as the text is 'destroyed' there is an increasing need and effort on the part of reader-oriented critics to redefine the aims and methods of literary study. The preoccupation with audience and interpretation is central to contemporary American and English reader-response criticism.

Feminist critics, here and in America, ask fairly similar questions but in alternative modes. Americans are concerned more with inscription. The questions here are: 'By what codes is the audience inscribed in the work?', 'How does an inscribed audience contribute to reading the text?' English feminists are concerned more with conventions. The question for them is: 'What conventions – aesthetic or cultural – do readers use in trying to make sense of texts and authors use in facilitating, or perhaps frustrating, readers' activities?'

In the process of reading and re-reading about male critics feminists have learned a good deal about the focus of literary meaning and what alternatives to tradition can be proposed. Earlier male critics like Wayne C. Booth and Walter Gibson evolved within the confines of a formalist position which assumes the value and uniqueness of the literary work of art. Semiotic and structuralist approaches in the work of Genette and Riffaterre developed the idea of the reader *in* the text and took the literary activity, not to be about assigning meaning as such, but about codes that make the text *readable*. Their analysis remains, however, firmly committed to the assumption of textual objectivity. The more phenomenological approach of Wolfgang Iser paid attention to the reader actively producing textual meaning. As with Norman Holland's Delphi seminars male critics have begun to relate people's reading experiences to their life experiences.

Continental theories have then been of use to both male and feminist American critics. In 'The Interpreter's Self' Walter Michaels suggests that American formalist and French post-structuralist attitudes toward the self have a common if un-acknowledged meeting-ground in American pragmatism. Michaels thus implicitly acknowledges the alternate model of the self that feminist literary critics have made. American males, Michaels argues, from the American pragmatist C.S. Pierce on, are frightened by the notion of an anarchist self. Feminists, on the other hand, as Hélène Cixous claims in 'The Laugh of the Medusa', *are* anarchic. Feminine texts pulsate with a rhetoric of rebellion and rupture.

Clearly it would be wrong to ignore the influences of particular critics such as Ricoeur, particular texts such as Barthes' *S/Z*, and particular stances such as Geoffrey Hartman's definition of reading as a dialogic and creative act, on feminist criticism. But there is a way in which the reader who emerges from those male critics has (for Booth and Gibson) no privileged status. He (and it is a he) takes a very abstract approach to reading (for Iser and Ricoeur). And for psychoanalytic critics like Holland he is the totally unified self dear to American ego psychology.

Feminist literary critics have used general human psychology like transactive criticism more to illuminate the *process* of reader reading. The pioneering work in the field of subjective criticism is Louise Rosenblatt's *Literature as Exploration*, written as long ago as 1938. She is the longest-writing American critic to use reader-response criticism and, from 1938, through the hegemony of New Criticism and structuralism, was developing a theory of reading which she calls transactional. Rosenblatt was influenced by John Dewey's notion of transaction as a two-way relationship of self-definition. Transaction equals a distinction between the text – the sequence of printed or voiced symbols – and the literary work which results from the conjunction of a reader and a text.

Although not a programmatic feminist (evident in her designation of the reader as 'he'), Rosenblatt is helpful to feminism in her instrumental use of criticism. She has extended her critique of the reading process to define aesthetic choice as the prerogative of the reader not the writer (Rosenblatt, 1981). A non-aesthetic reading she calls efferent (from the Latin *efferre* – to carry away). In this activity the reader's attention is centred on what will be retained *after* the reading event (like reading medicine labels). In an aesthetic reading, the focus of the reader is on what she is living through during the reading event. Criticism, to Rosenblatt, is therefore an *efferent* activity since it points to syntactic patterns or whatever else we may want to carry away. But Rosenblatt does not really give an answer to how we *should* experience reading. She is locked within American individualism. As she puts it, 'essential to transaction is a particular reader, a particular human being'.

An American feminist critic who uses what we can call the

efferent approach is Judith Fetterley. Fetterley chooses literary works which can represent particular male emotions, like a fear of sexuality or growing up, and she itemises male literature as a series of designs on a reader. Her authors are Washington Irving, Sherwood Anderson, Nathaniel Hawthorne and William Faulkner, and her aim is to deal with the problem of entry (of a woman reader) into texts of male characters. Fetterley herself represents a crucial feature of American feminist criticism. The book claims to be about sexual politics but it is really about the culture of sexuality without any materialist analysis. The problem of course is circular. Fetterley cannot deal with the specifics of women characters – their economic context – because she has answered herself in the beginning by assuming that women characters in male texts are there as products of male sickness. Not all males are phallic critics, just as not all phallic critics are male. To an English critic Fetterley's might seem a very unproblematic reading of literature where characters are people only in terms of their feelings and motives.

Kate Millett in *Sexual Politics* is another American woman reader. She confronted literature as the record of the collective consciousness of patriarchy (Millett, 1971). The book was a revelation of sexism and woman-hating in the work of D.H. Lawrence, Mailer and Miller and revolutionised the way women and men were reading, or misreading contemporary literature.

Where Fetterley looks at male emotions Millett took her writers to be archetypes of particular *social* values within capitalism – the values of violence, sexuality and the cash nexus. As Norman Mailer gleefully pointed out, Kate Millett is an annoying critic – and not just to Mailer. She paraphrases at length, confuses author with character, and generalises to make all-inclusive points. Reading Kate Millett *now* is a little like watching black and white television after years of colour. But her faults come, I think, from not knowing her audience. Millett lacked what is now a feminist constituency and she was trying to create one. Hence her time with lesser fiction where sexist themes and techniques are more explicit.

Millett is a very moral critic and a very moral writer. Millett's career has been a total continuum of fiction and criticism. We can read *Sita* or *Sexual Politics* as a balance between narrative and interrogative moral debates. Both in her fiction and in her criticism Millett helps us to a 'lived-through' experience. In *Sita* life and art are interdependent. The narrator's relationship with Sita has to end so that her journal can. It is difficult to impose 'efferent' readings on Millett since she refuses imposed structural patterns as in the juxtaposed columns of her prostitute papers (Millett, 1971). The hatred of realism evident in the *text* of *Sita* – its unstable narrator and her uses of imagistic, repetitive monologues are joined by a hatred of the real in its *content* – in both characters' preference for photographs, scrapbooks and personal notes rather than real events. In *Sita* Millett gives us the all-American woman, 'all the women I never was', just as in her criticism she demolishes the all-American male.

Kate Millett in *Sexual Politics*, Louise Rosenblatt and Judith Fetterley have stressed the relationships between texts and readers while remaining very individualistic, and hence very American, critics. English feminists, particularly in the work of the Birmingham Centre for Cultural Studies, see their responsibility more to the constituency of women readers that Millett helped to create. To English feminists, critics should choose to work with designated groups of women readers sharing, rather than describing, critical tools. Criticism, from this position, must question the relation between cultural and other practices not as a series of artefacts but as a lived experience of its readers (Hall *et al.*, 1980).

The Birmingham Centre took a quite novel concern with 'the popular' in a radically new sense, producing concrete research on ideas of the popular and their interaction with women from different classes. Methodologically this led English feminist literary criticism to its more ethnographic approach, moving from the formal text to its lived reception. 'Women, feminism and literature in the 1930s' and the study of Barbara Cartland and Winifred Holtby in *Culture, Media and Language* does not consider texts *per se* but looks at the process of literary production and the interpellation of, or hailing of, readers by texts. The Birmingham Centre approach reads popular narratives like Barbara Cartland's *Blue Heather* in a search for motifs (of home and marriage) which can be related to social concerns. The Birmingham Centre has pioneered a collective approach both to research methods in general, and to reader groups within literary criticism. It has mapped different cultural practices and aimed to mobilise them. In Britain feminism has been inter-connected with the reconstitution of 'community' in an active involvement in women's writing groups creating a tradition outside the formally academic, as in the women's groups 'Human Voices' and 'Commonplace Workshop' (Worpole, 1982).

Although a radical departure in feminist literary criticism the movement suffers from anti-formalism. For example, another way of reading the romance texts would be to use deconstruction's view of the text as a set of relations with other texts. This provides as helpful a model for reader-response criticism of romance where moral norms are as much to do with readers' expectations of form (four-letter words are added to *Women's Weekly* romances on appearance in book form to attract a wider readership) as with the Birmingham link of reader expectation with *lived* experience.

In reader-response criticism (as with cultural criticism and concepts of difference) there are clear divergent English and American styles. English feminists are interested in collective evaluation. Relocating meaning first in the reader's self and then in community strategies that constitute it, English feminists have re-politicised literary criticism. Americans too share a view of language as a form of power but a power for reading women as academic individuals set apart from the merely practical spheres of women's lives.

Conclusion

As this article indicates, feminist criticism in both America and England is a continual and creative source of argument, debate and resistance. Neither country has dictated a single constraining ideology of criticism but there are clearly two different visions, for English and Americans, of the function, forms and methods of feminist literary criticism. English feminists have tried to define women's relationships to themselves in terms of class, historical context and those as representations in literary form. American feminists have tried to define women in terms of personal history, notions of difference and theories of identity.

111

The critical tools and disciplinary influences are similarly varied. English feminists prefer a thematic textual approach around the key concepts of domesticity or marriage. American feminists' debt to rhetoric and psychoanalysis enables them to a more experimental linguistic reading of generative terms.

Any attempt to define all feminist criticism, then, in terms of one distinctive method is doomed to failure. Perhaps feminist criticism means simply any kind of writing about women from the point of view of women. We should celebrate both American and English critical methods rather than certificating or non-certificating women as to whether they speak the discourse of feminism better or worse. I hope my comparison of feminist critics and techniques will enable us as critical readers to continue with a fuller understanding of each other's methods and a clearer sense of sharing our critical tools. My intention, in other words, is not to add to the feminist critics I have examined in this chapter a feminist critique of my own. Rather I would like to pose a question.

The final test of any literary theory to Terry Eagleton is: 'How would it work with Joyce's *Finnegan's Wake*?' (Eagleton, 1983). Feminists might prefer to test out their critical technique by asking: 'How would it work with Djuna Barnes?' *Nightwood* is a deliberate parody of social and moral norms to show the impossibility of precise gender definitions. Barnes' women are repositories of pre-social experiences. Static characters, they act as representative myths in an intensely analogical, condensed fairy tale. How would English feminists feel about a writer who only uses depravity to catch a sense of the past?

The 'difference' between American and English feminist criticism is then a difference *within* feminism. There is no better or worse method in literary critical terms. Feminist criticism needs to interweave these two kinds of temporality – the American contemporary cursive time and the English sense of a longer cultural past in a *dynamic* of signs. Feminist criticism *is* gradually freeing itself from ethnocentrism, homophobia *and* now hopefully, from chauvinism.

Notes

1. In 'Sexual/Textual Politics' Tori Moi describes aspects of Anglo-American feminist criticism (in F. Barker *et al.*, *The Politics of Theory*, University of Essex Press, Colchester, 1983). While a helpful account of some theoretical assumptions, Moi's allegiance to Kristéva leads her to denigrate Anglo-American criticism as if it were a homogeneous entity. By refusing to see the complexities in each country's mode of criticism, Moi unfairly attacks Anglo-Americans as humanist empiricists.

Bibliography

This bibliography is a selection of useful and representative contemporary feminist criticism. It supplies background references for this chapter and is not intended to be an exhaustive list. That more extensive collection will be in Maggie Humm, *Feminist Criticism* (Harvester Press, forthcoming).

E. Abel, *Writing and Sexual Difference* (Harvester Press, Brighton, 1982)

C.J. Allen, 'Feminist(s) Reading: A Response to Elaine Showalter', in Abel, op. cit.

N. Auerbach, *Communities of Women* (Harvard University Press, Cambridge, Mass., 1978)

H. Baehr, 'The Impact of Feminism on Media Studies – Just Another Commercial Break?', in *Men's Studies Modified*, ed. D. Spender (Pergamon Press, Oxford, 1981)

M. Barrett, *Women and Writing* (Women's Press, London, 1979) 'Feminism and Cultural Politics', in *Feminism, Culture and Politics*, ed. R. Brunt and C. Rowan (Lawrence & Wishart, London 1982)

C. Belsey, 'Re-reading the Great Tradition', in *Rereading English*, ed. P. Widdowson (Methuen, London 1982)

H. Bloom, *The Anxiety of Influence* (Oxford University Press, Oxford, 1979)

C. Buck, 'Freud and H.D.: bisexuality and a feminine discourse', *M/F*, 8 (1983)

E. Bulkin, 'Heterosexism and Women's Studies', *Radical Teacher*, N17 (1980)

—— *Lesbian Fiction* (Persephone Press, Watertown, Mass., 1981)

—— *Lesbian Poetry* (Persephone Press, Watertown, Mass., 1981)

J. Chicago, *The Dinner Party* (Anchor Books, New York, 1979)

S.K. Cornillon, *Images of Women in Fiction* (Bowling Green University Popular Press, Bowling Green, Ohio, 1972)

R. Coward, 'Are Women's Novels Feminist Novels?', *Feminist Review*, N5 (1980).

'Sexual Politics and Psychoanalysis', in Brunt, op. cit.

T. Eagleton, *Literary Theory* (Basil Blackwell, Oxford, 1983)

M. Ellman, *Thinking About Women* (Harcourt Brace Jovanovich, New York, 1968)

M. Evans, *Work on Women: A Guide to the Literature* (Tavistock Press, London, 1979)

J. Fetterley, *The Resisting Reader* (Indiana University Press, Indiana, 1978)

B. Fisher, 'What is Feminist Pedagogy?', *Radical Teacher*, N18 (1979)

E. Fox-Genovese, 'The New Female Literary Culture', *Antioch Review*, V38 (1980)

J. Gallop, *Feminism and Psychoanalysis* (Macmillan, London, 1982).

J.K. Gardiner, 'On Female Identity and Writing by Women', in Abel, op. cit.

J.K. Gardiner *et al.*, 'An Interchange on Feminist Criticism on Dancing Through the Minefield', *Feminist Studies*, 8, N3 (1982)

S.M. Gilbert and S. Gubar, *The Madwoman in The Attic* (Yale University Press, New Haven, 1979)

S. Hall *et al.*, *Culture, Media, Language* (Hutchinson, London, 1980)

E. Hardwick, *Seduction and Betrayal* (Random House, New York, 1974)

G. Hartman (ed.), *Literature and Psychoanalysis* (John S. Hopkins Press, Baltimore, 1978)

S. Heath, 'Sexual Difference and Representation', *Screen*, V19, N3 (1978)

F. Howe, 'Breaking the Disciplines', in *The Structure of Knowledge*, ed. B. Reed (Great Lakes Colleges Association Women's Studies, Ann Arbor, Michigan, 1978)

G. Hull, 'Rewriting Afro-American Literature', *Radical Teacher*, N6, 1977

M. Jacobus (ed.), *Women Writing and Writing About Women* (Croom Helm, London, 1979)

E. Jelinek (ed.), *Women's Autobiography* (Indiana University Press, Bloomington, 1980)

C. Kaplan, 'Wild Nights: Pleasure/Sexuality/Feminism', in *Formations of Pleasure*, (Routledge & Kegan Paul, London 1983)

A. Kolodny, 'Dancing Through the Minefield: some observations of the theory, practice and politics of a feminist literary criticism', *Feminist Studies*, 6, N1 (1980)

J. Kristéva, 'Women's Time', *Signs* V7, N1 (1981)

A. Kuhn, *Women's Pictures; Feminism and Cinema* (Routledge & Kegan Paul, London, 1982)

L. Lippard, *From the Center* (E.P. Dutton, New York, 1976)

T. Lovell, 'Writing Like A Woman: A Question of Politics', in *The Politics of Theory*, ed. F. Barker *et al.* (University of Essex Press, Colchester, 1983)

A. MacRobbie (ed.), *Feminism for Girls* (Routledge & Kegan Paul, London, 1981)

Marxist-Feminist Literature Collective, 'Women's Writing. *Jane Eyre, Shirley, Villette, Aurora Leigh*', *Ideology and Consciousness*, N3 (1978)

M.G. Mason and C.H. Green (eds), *Journeys: Autobiographical Writings of Women* (G.K. Hall & Co., Boston, 1979)

K. Millett, *Sexual Politics* (Virago, London, 1977),

—— 'Prostitution', in *Woman in Sexist Society*, ed. V Gornick and B.K. Moran (Basic Books, New York, 1971)

J. Mitchell and A. Oakley (eds), *The Rights and Wrongs of Women* (Penguin, Harmondsworth, 1976)

E. Moers, *Literary Women* (Anchor Books, New York, 1977)

J. Montefiore, 'Feminist Identity and the Poetic Tradition', *Feminist Review*, N13, (1983)

A. Ostriker, 'Body Language', in *The State of the Language*, ed. L. Michaels and C. Ricks (University of California Press, Berkeley, 1980)

A Rich, *Of Woman Born* (Virago, London, 1977)

—— *On Lies, Secrets and Silences* (Virago, London, 1980).

—— 'Compulsory Heterosexuality and Lesbian Existence', in *The Signs: Reader Women, Gender and Scholarship*, ed. E.K. Abel (University of Chicago Press, 1983)

L. Rosenblatt, *Literature as Exploration* (Appleton-Century, New York, 1938).

—— 'On the Aesthetic as the Basic Model of the Reading Process', *Bucknell Review*, V26, N1 (1981)

S. Rowbotham, *Women's Consciousness, Man's World* (Penguin, London, 1973)

E. Showalter, 'Towards a Feminist Poetics' in Jacobus, op. cit.

—— *A Literature of Their Own* (Virago, London, 1978).

—— 'Feminist Criticism in the Wilderness', in Abel, op. cit.

A. Snitow *et al.* (eds), *Desire, the Politics of Sexuality* (Virago, London, 1984)

P.M. Spacks, *The Female Imagination* (Knopf, New York, 1977)

G. Spivak, 'Unmaking and Making in *To The Lighthouse*', in *Women and Language in Literature and Society*, ed. S. McConnell-Ginet *et al.* (Praeger, New York, 1980)

G. Stewart, *A New Mythos* (Eden Press, Vermont, 1979)

Women's Writing

P. Stubbs, *Women and Fiction* (Methuen, London, 1981)
R. Williams, *Keywords* (Fontana, London, 1976)
J. Williamson, *Decoding Advertisements* (Marion Boyars, London, 1978)
K. Worpole, *The Republic of Letters* (Comedia Press, London, 1982)

6

WOMEN TALKING ABOUT WRITING

Sue Roe and Emma Tennant

Preface

The dialogue which follows is the slightly edited and abridged transcript of a conversation between Emma Tennant and me which was completely unprepared and spontaneous, and represents our first meeting.

Moira Monteith and I had decided to invite Emma to make a contribution to the volume as we felt that her work raises, within a wholly creative framework, important feminist and literary issues with significant bearing on the issues discussed throughout this volume. Emma felt she would prefer to do so in the form of a discussion with a fellow writer and I was suggested as an admiring reader of Emma's work and a writer.

We met, then, with no preparation and no pre-arranged format, to talk informally and to discuss our writing and reading, and talked breathlessly and without stopping, as I think this transcription suggests, for about two hours. What emerges for me out of the transcription is the immediacy and directness with which we were able to confront each other with views and questions, and the clarity of the issues which surface even when we speak in broken and interrupted sentences and offer each other either half-formed or sometimes very detailed or specific thoughts. Issues seem to emerge on a large scale carrying with them wide repercussions, even when they are broached in the most cursory of ways.

The mysteriousness and the compulsion of the writing process becomes an increasingly urgent issue as the conversation progresses: both of us seem to want to express the extent to which writing is a driving force and to which issues emerge and are shaped at various succeeding stages in the writing process, even when – as often for Emma – these seem to be initiated by reading the work of another writer. Writing about feminist issues emerges as a practice inextricably bound up with the process of another, almost primeval practice, that of writing 'itself': simply, the desire to express creative drives and energies. It is difficult, always, to pinpoint which emerges first: the impulse, or the issue.

We were, I hope it will be remembered, talking very informally in the process of compiling this piece – often quite a difficult thing to do, and I am sure that the issues which emerge out of our conversation would have emerged in quite different shapes and forms had we prepared written contributions in the place of or as a sequel to what follows. But it is not necessarily the case that, had we presented written papers, we would have focused on different issues, nor that the issues would have emerged in our respective minds in a different order of priority. The 'text' of our piece emerges, then, out of *dialogue*, and we have retained its form because we like the degree of fluency which it has given us. It also means, I think, that we were able to be diverse, spontaneous, and to find ourselves confronting issues which may just possibly have been held in check by the process of writing and re-writing.

What follows, then, is in some ways the kind of kaleidoscopic collision of ideas, issues, desires, anxieties, pleasures, which confront a writer prior to writing. At the same time, we are talking as writers with the experiences of re-drafting and publication behind us, and – again, importantly – as readers. The transcription of our dialogue is revealing, then, of some of the ways in which women not only think spontaneously but also *talk* to each other, as well as of the ways in which women write, and it is as such that this contribution takes its place among the work presented by the community of women writers and critics represented in this volume.

Sue Roe

Moira Monteith: Has the fact that you are a woman and a writer made any difference to you both?

Emma Tennant: Yes. I would say, really, an enormous difference, because I think there is a different way of looking at things and I think it's very difficult to define what it is. But I would think that one of the great dangers at the moment is a ghettoisation, precisely, that is happening with a woman writer and that is a very difficult problem to confront. Women have, of course, always written, particularly because of it being an easier thing to scribble in the corner of the room than to afford a studio or go out and sculpt or become a musician. And, of course, some of the best English writers have been women. So that a kind of self-consciousness, which I think is important now, also has its bad side, and can make women closed off from other things that are happening, and from other perceptions, in the world, and closed off by men, in a bad way by identifying themselves – it seems to me – too much as being 'a woman writer'. I don't know what Sue feels about this?

Sue Roe: I think, in *Estella*, I didn't realise at all, until it was long written, to what extent I was responding in thinking of it in the first place to a sort of stereotyped, female imagery. Because at the centre of *Estella* for me now is the very, very potent image of Miss Havisham and Estella and the notion of time, locking and standing still, and the image of two women both arrested somehow, and hidden from history. And the sense of powerlessness that this has on the face of it, but once you're inside a structure like that, the sense of something terribly potent and actually quite powerful, but which, when you look at it from outside that framework, just doesn't count for very much at all, that you can actually explain in feminist terms.

Emma Tennant: I think it's worth women writing, when they know that that's what they're doing. So I'm really only making a very general point, that there are dangers of specific women's publishing presses, and so on.

Moira Monteith: What sort of dangers?

Emma Tennant: I think the dangers are – of being pushed outside the human race, which women always have been, in another specially brilliant way done by women themselves.

Sue Roe: Absolutely.

Emma Tennant: And this is the final double-think of the whole thing. I do think that Virago and The Women's Press doing all these reprints has been a brilliant thing, and the discovery of these hidden people and hidden lives has, on the whole, been really wonderful. I started rather late, when I was 34, eleven years ago, and there was no question of there being such a thing as a woman writer then, which is rather amazing. In 1973, which was when my first book *The Time of the Crack* came out, from the point of view of writing, of actual creative writing and publishing, as far as I know, there wasn't that kind of division: Who are you? Are you a writer or a woman writer?

Sue Roe: But did those essentially external divisions actually affect your imaginative power and your imaginative style?

Emma Tennant: Yes. I think they did. And in some ways, I regret it. I think it's been almost impossible for a women writer – well it would be impossible historically – to avoid the self-consciousness which has come from the, quite right, rise of the movement. So that it is impossible, for instance, for me to say, whether I would have written *The Bad Sister* and then *Queen of Stones*, had it not been for a greater and greater self-consciousness. This I don't think does apply with women writers, who actually, funnily

120

enough, are not called women writers, like Anita Brookner and Edna O'Brien. You'll find that a woman writer is usually considered to be somebody who has looked at the whole feminist issue, is usually sympathetic to it, and is trying to get through, if possible, to a younger audience – that's how I see it anyway – and, by using creative writing, make various points. There are, of course, many writers who are women who are very much not like that, who show in their novels that feminism is a silly, trivial, stupid thing and who are, as far as I know, never described as women writers.

Sue Roe: Presumably your decision with regard to a change of style in approach and narrative perspective in *Woman Beware Woman* reflects that anxiety, but actually, it seems to me that what emerges in *Woman Beware Woman* is your sense of a number of layers of narrative all working together. A number of stories, conflicting and co-existing, and the notion of a kind of metamorphosis in Minnie which one can take for its own sake, not as a feminist issue. You're talking about the way minds work.

Emma Tennant: Yes. *Woman Beware Woman* is exactly – you're quite right to say – a reaction against going into a rather self-conscious mould. I felt that if I wanted to portray the American feminist journalist in an unsympathetic way then I was jolly well going to, and therefore I made her rather a stereotype. But I felt rather leant on, more by my own beliefs you see. Really the theory must never stand in the way of creativity. When it comes down to people writing books in which there are things like anti-Semitism or racism – I just cannot answer what I think about that. Somebody like Céline is a most terrible man, and the most fascinating writer to read. I would find that if he was censored from the point of view of people reading literature, there would be an impoverishment.

Sue Roe: It's to do with myth as well. I thought that in *Queen of Stones* what emerged was actually the importance of myth, which the psychoanalyst tries to put the full-stop on early, by discounting the Leda and Swan image.

Emma Tennant: I think that what I'm trying to say after all, is that the figures of authority in *Queen of Stones,* by ignoring myth and imagination, insisting on the rational way of thinking (the psychoanalyst or the churchman or whatever, the bishop in *Queen of Stones* who won't have much to do with anything funny happening, he might do a quick exorcism and so on) by that denial the troubles of the world are unleashed. I suppose it's a simple message.

Sue Roe: They didn't clue into the myth. It seems to me, what you're doing particularly in *Queen of Stones* and in *Woman Beware Woman* – which to me are the two of your novels that belong together – is actually something more akin to psychoanalysis where you're dealing with a personal myth set off against a personal history, set off against a common experience –

Emma Tennant: What do you call a personal myth? You mean one of the character's personal myths or mine?

Sue Roe: One of the character's.

Emma Tennant: So you mean, in *Woman Beware Woman* Minnie's myth is the family to which she thought she belonged?

Sue Roe: Yes.

Emma Tennant: And then what happens when you believe something and it turns out not to be true?

Sue Roe: Exactly. Because there's an amazing *volte-face* which ... well, I needed to read that one twice because I could really feel the almost insidious power of the changeabout at the end.

Emma Tennant: Actually somebody else did it, in my first draft.

	Yes, I couldn't bring myself to make it her. I knew it was her really, but I simply would not accept it, so I made it Fran, who went out shooting with a camera. You know, a rather cliché thing but actually did it – by mistake – was engineered to do it.
Sue Roe:	The shock of the ending actually is not that she kills a man, but that we have trusted her, very faithfully, and that maybe it was wrong to trust her. Maybe she wasn't a character we could actually trust.
Emma Tennant:	That's of course the unreliable narrator, isn't it?
Sue Roe:	Yes. She's your first character who actually bears the full weight of the responsibility of the narrator, isn't she?
Emma Tennant:	Yes, she is.
Sue Roe:	You have a separate narrator for all your others.
Emma Tennant:	That's right.
Sue Roe:	Actually your stories generate other stories, because *The Bad Sister* made me wonder at what stage you'd added the reportage. I wondered whether that came first or last.
Emma Tennant:	Afterwards.
Sue Roe:	I wondered. The only reason I could come up with for your not being able to leave Jane's narrative by itself – because it seemed to me that that was a novel by itself – was that it probably couldn't support the weight of the comment you wanted to make about the potentially insidious nature of separatist feminism.
Emma Tennant:	I think that was true, but it really was based on *The Confessions of a Justified Sinner* by James Hogg. A great Scottish classic. Always fascinates me that although it comes out in one form or another it doesn't go south of the border. I come from where Hogg actually lived and therefore it's not strange to me. Now, one of

the reasons he's not travelled south is because of his interest in the double. He was the first person who brought the double to English – in fact, Scottish – literature. Because the German metaphysicians, basically Hoffmann, etc., brought the double in and it caught in Scotland. Hogg was the first, then obviously Jekyll and Hyde, and so on. And there have been various theories put forward, some of them by Karl Miller in *Cockburn's Millennium* which I think is a very interesting book about the judge Lord Cockburn, as to why Scotland would be particularly fertile ground for the double. Some of them being that a lot of people in Scotland speak Lallans or whatever as small children and then have to speak English. That Scotland is obviously colonised by England, and therefore breeds a totally different kind of literature, more romantic, more akin to European literature and European imagination than England ever has. I, of course, find all this very interesting and provocative as it's where I happen to come from and where my imagination – it seems to me – is so completely unlike a lot of English novelists. But, in fact, you're quite right, I started with the journal of Jane Wild, and then I realised I must do as Hogg had done, to give it this balance and in my case to put in this kind of male judging voice.

Moira Monteith: Would you equate some sort of authority, sometimes imperial in terms of ... well, what England has become, with the male voice?

Emma Tennant: Yes.

Moira Monteith: Because you do seem very often to have this frame that Sue was talking about.

Sue Roe: And isn't there also some neurotic sense in which women's voices, on their own, can become so carried away, can just go wild, can just go off into that wilderness ...?

Emma Tennant: Can be taken as babble?

Sue Roe:	Yes, and just get out of control. The things you say about the double interest me because there is all that, and there's some other kind of power of the double, which is particularly related to women and women's consciousness – and women's biology. It seems to me that the double appears for you, almost always, at the point of adolescence. There starts to become a choice, about who you might become, as a woman.
Emma Tennant:	Yes. Then there are the two kinds of creativity. You're mostly told, it's just enough to have a baby, and that is your creativity. So, one of the reasons I wrote *The Bad Sister* was taking up Virginia Woolf's idea, that a woman has another woman in her, and the two are warring. And also, my idea of the muse having to be female, and the male poet calling down this muse whenever he feels like it, and the woman calls down another woman, who gives her a nasty kick on the shin. I thought this would be an amusing thing to do, but most of all, to look at the effects of extreme – really like a Manson thing – is what I was basing it on. Where at that point, that very extremist feminism ('Kill your father because he is paternalistic capitalism') that was the nearest thing now to that form of Calvinist repression which Hogg was dealing with.
Sue Roe:	And you're always doing a dual thing, I think.
Emma Tennant:	Yes, It seems to happen a very great deal. I just don't know enough about why it should. I think it happens a lot with poets. It certainly happened a lot with Sylvia Plath when she's writing about the colours. You look back at something you've done and it's all been red and white, and that's when you've been trying to conjure up a certain kind of schizophrenic state, say, in the part of Jane Wild or whatever your heroine's in. And whilst one has not been

125

	consciously copying her – I find all that beyond any kind of rational discussion.
Sue Roe:	I always think that unless a thing is beyond any kind of rational discussion, you can't write it because that's where the creative impulse comes from, actually.
Emma Tennant:	Yes.
Sue Roe:	And that you either feed the theory in gradually or you can read the theory back, when you've done it. That's the way it works, isn't it?
Emma Tennant:	I think so. Yes.
Sue Roe:	Do you think you are pitting against something very mysterious and something ...
Emma Tennant:	Yes. I notice with your writing, it has a tremendous amount of colour in it. Which is something I do think sometimes about women's writing. There does seem to be a way in which women see colours with greater sensitivity. Anyway, your writing has very strong colour and sensuality, as indeed had Colette.
Sue Roe:	Colette was a very formative influence, as was Virginia Woolf, of course.
Moira Monteith:	Don't you think that language has something to do with it? Women apparently use more shades when they talk about colours. I was thinking about the language and what Nicole Jouve has written, and you did say that coming from Scotland made a difference. That it perhaps began this sense of a double.
Emma Tennant:	In terms of language? I think so. As I said, I was very interested in Karl Miller and Edwin Morgan's particular comments and essays, on the possibility that this feeling of a double in Scotland came from being a different person as a child, to what you had to be as a grown-up, so you were speaking, either another language altogether, like Lallans, or in my case I spoke in a very broad Scots dialect. I didn't leave there at all until I was 9½, and I was at a

village school with six other children. Anyway that is quite a long time to stay in one place without ever moving and indeed it's been very hard for me to adjust to the outside world as the place I was in was this valley cul-de-sac, I never left it; and going out of it was a nasty shock. But I think in general that's what does make Scottish people feel odd, that they then have to come to terms with the fact that they are really English, once they are grown-up, and are getting jobs. And Scotland is a backward, feudal country, there's no doubt. It is a disaster, Scotland, and most Scottish people who can bear to face it do think so, I think. It's very hard to be optimistic up there.

Sue Roe: You're also talking, as well, about the language of sensuality because that's where you were a child, being very wild and free and presumably able to be sensual, in a way that wasn't at all thwarted or restricted. Coming to London, one of the changes was trying to socialise and politicise your thinking. For me, the use of colour, I think, and the use of sensual imagery was a way of just creating a sensual landscape, which I could create in fiction, which hadn't existed for me before until the time during which I was writing that book.

Emma Tennant: I can tell, reading your books, that you haven't decided, 'I am now going to create a sensual atmosphere'. It came and therefore it is the book. I think Jean Rhys said that Ford Maddox Ford had said to her, 'Don't have anything to do with atmosphere'. Your thing is like a marvellous piece of material. It's shot through with various, threads but if one started to think, how am I going to put colour or warmth or something into it, then it sticks out, doesn't it, a mile? But *vis à vis* language. I mean, obviously it's very unlike what Nicole Jouve must feel, and honestly, I have such admiration for her translations of her own work. But it's quite a different thing. I think Scotland is more the small country that's been colonised by England, which of course is not true with France at all. So I think it is probably rather a different matter.

Moira Monteith: But you are talking about somebody belonging to two cultures?

Emma Tennant: Yes, definitely.

Moira Monteith: And having to forget one which, in all sorts of ways, is terribly important to you, not merely in the way that you spoke but everything that you associated with it?

Emma Tennant: Quite. What's that – 'Caledonia, stern and wild,/Fit nurse for a poetic child'?

Sue Roe: You've already expressed your scepticism about thinking in terms of being a woman writer, but doesn't that notion of having two cultures come back again to being a woman, doesn't it work on that level of having to balance two kinds of framework, two kinds of thinking?

Emma Tennant: What I really mean is, that I wouldn't want anyone to be thought of as a woman writer in the way that only other women would read them. The point would be to hope to reach young boys, men, seventeen or eighteen, the kind of people who would automatically read J. G. Ballard or whatever, and who would get a feeling and understanding of what one was trying to put across. And while it might be all very nice if we just read each other I think it would be a tremendous sadness to discover that that was just one's only readership. And the more it's – well, ghettoised is a rotten word – but the more all these women understand each other and they know what they're putting over, the harder it's going to be to do the most important thing of all, which is to get men's consciousness tuned in to the things that have been cut out of their education, really, for such a long time and particularly in the last 200 to 300 years.

Moira Monteith: Did you have any break in the way you spoke at all, Sue?

Emma Tennant: Where did you grow up?

Sue Roe: I grew up in Leicester, but I went to a church school so I spoke an ordinary kind of English without any accent. But I went to France for the first time when I was about fourteen and it made a great impression on me. And I played the piano, as a child. That's what I thought I would do. I think I thought I would be a pianist. And music came far easier and earlier than writing for me. I never wrote as a child. The first time I really seriously put pen to paper was when I started *Estella*. But I was musical and I loved speaking French because of the sense in which you lose one personality and take up another. I found that fascinating – it was like acting. And when I came to write, it felt a bit like speaking French; however fluent you are, there's a kind of gap between the thought and the vocabulary – or the language – available to you.

Emma Tennant: Did you feel you'd become French?

Sue Roe: Yes. I think I wanted to be French, for a a while. When I left school I went to Switzerland and spoke French for a year, and did a bit of writing but nothing that really worked.

Moira Monteith: Why do you think you wanted to learn French so much? Is it liberating?

Sue Roe: Very. It enables me to feel and think things I can't feel and think in English: like writing, which produces feelings and thoughts you don't otherwise have. There's a 'writing consciousness' which, when I write – which doesn't just mean when I'm actually writing – there's a way of being in your writing language, when you're not even writing. Sometimes you feel

yourself to be in touch with your writing consciousness. Then I feel I'm thinking about
things my own way, and also that there are
certain kinds of rapport going on with Virginia
Woolf and Colette and Emma Tennant and
Eva Figes and other people with whom you
feel a kind of solidarity. But also that excludes
all kinds of other people, not just men: I mean,
it's a particular style of thinking. I don't know
whether it's necessarily a female way of thinking, but there your historical links come in,
and your social links and political links.

Moira Monteith: Emma has said that the narration in *Queen of
Stones* is enclosed within male language.

Sue Roe: Yes. Girded by it. Although I don't think
that necessarily means 'language spoken by
men'. Not literally. I thought that only women
would like *Estella*, for instance and I was surprised to find that half the people who liked
Estella were men. And I can't explain that,
actually. I suppose it does say something that I
was surprised.

Moira Monteith: Why did you think women would like it?

Sue Roe: I think because ... I'll tell you what I think
about it really. I think it was a very irrespons-
ible thing to write. A male friend of mine
recently said that one of the problems he had
with *Estella* is that it has no historical or
political perspective. And I mentioned this to
a feminist critic who threw up her hands in
horror and said that that was surely the whole
point of it. That its sense of being hidden from
history, and its wholly interiorised point of
view, was the historical and political point. I
wasn't at all sure of how interiorised it was
when I was writing it though. I thought I was
just narrating events. But the fact that Estella
even managed not to have any history what-
soever now seems to me to be very feminist. I
did feel, writing it, that it represented a kind of

escape world which I actually managed to inhabit for a year, and wrote about. At the end of the story, Estella gets back on the train with her folder and goes off to do a job. She gets back on the rails again. And I did feel a bit guilty about that, as though it had all been a kind of foray or just an adventure, into the world of sensuality, really sensuality disconnected from politics, or history or society. I think that's another feminist issue. I think it's Foucault who says that the belief that your sexual and sensual life is separate from your political and social life is actually a comment on your history and your politics. I think I wanted to exploit that separation really, and I think that that particular separation is something that women tend to be very interested in, and something that men tend not to be able to relate to.

Moira Monteith: You were talking about the personal myth. Would you call this sense of enclosure, of two women being close together, a personal myth?

Sue Roe Yes. I think I probably carry around with me a sense that there's a layer of the life I'm leading that's totally hidden from all the other surface lives.

Emma Tennant: I was reading only two days ago a collection by Audrey Lorde. She's a black Grenadian poet, but she lives in America, and apart from being a fascinating poet, has written a collection of essays and speeches in which she's talking to Adrienne Rich, and discussing the black mother in everyone, and the importance of not thinking that it's just in women, but in fact that it is in everyone and has been eradicated, mostly in white men, and how the important thing is to try and recover - what she calls the black mother - this poetic voice. And she's not at all pretentious. I thought she

131

was fascinating and very intelligent, a very nice woman. But I think that what's happened with me so far, is trying to show that an imaginative voice, which often gets out of control, because there's no structure to help the imagination of the woman, will run into a kind of – not exactly psycho babble – but into a sort of schizophrenic state, because of not having any power or control. It's then commented on cruelly by somebody paid by the establishment in one way or another, by a newspaper or television and so on, putting that voice in its place. It seems to me that someone can have feelings of powerlessness and extremely rational thoughts at the same time. I tried this very much with Minnie. I thought, 'Can I get away with this?' And then, 'Of course I can, it's me, everybody feels like this.' I sometimes decide that I want to make a remark about what's going on in the Soviet Union and what I think about this. Other times I may be spinning off into feelings of resentment or unhappiness like I think women particularly do.

Sue Roe: But wasn't that tension between powerlessness and rationale the thing that drove her to the ultimate, destructive acts? Isn't that tension terribly dangerous?

Emma Tennant: I think it is a dangerous tension, it probably either ends in a murder or in suicide or in the madhouse. I do think so.

Sue Roe: Or in submission? That's another choice.

Emma Tennant: Or in submission. But it was triggered off so much really by Moura, that she engineered it. The plot comes from the novella by Mérimée, *Colomba*, where the wild sister is standing at the harbour in Corsica and saying to the young man, 'Our father's been murdered, you will avenge his honour.' And the young man saying, 'Wait a minute, I'm modern. I'm from the

132

modern world,' and she says 'No, no, the vendetta's on' and she has engineered him into a right and a left. He kills two brigands, his future's finished as a soldier, as a person who does belong to the new, modern, I suppose Napoleonic, world. And I thought instead of using, of course, a sister, I would make it a mother. But that was the kind of structure that ran through it.

Sue Roe: Mothers, I feel in your work, are very potent, very dangerous people. She wasn't so much of a mother as some of your other mothers. The important thing about Moura was that she was an artist, and she cared as much about the fact that there was a change in her art at this point, as she did about getting somebody to avenge the death of her husband. The stabbing, much more graphic art she had started to do was very important to her.

Emma Tennant: That was very important to her. Funny you should say about her not being so much of a real mother. I had a great many thoughts about the title.

Sue Roe: I wanted to ask whether it was you or your editor who made up the title, because it seemed to me an intriguing title for the book.

Emma Tennant: When I was thinking of the book, before I'd even written it, I was speaking to Angela Carter on the telephone, and I said, 'I can't think of a title', and she said, 'Why don't you call it *Woman Beware Woman*?' I didn't go and read the Middleton play, *Women Beware Women*, which obviously Angela knew and I didn't. But, funnily enough, as these things always seem to consist of connections and coincidences, I read a review of a production of the play which said that the last lines are, 'It was all to do with lust and forgetfulness', which actually, the book, in fact, is to do with. It is to do with memory and slips of memory and forgetfulness, and indeed lust, because of her longings for Philip.

Moira Monteith: Sue said the mothers are very powerful. I didn't think in *The Bad Sister* that the mother was.

Emma Tennant: She was in a way, because Mrs Martin was also Meg. She was the most conventional nightmarish, Knightsbridge sort of lady, who in fact carried a vast load of repressed power and evil and really, jinxed poor Jane. When she made all these, of course, it was meant to be a joke, all these mayonnaises, she actually killed her, she sucked the life out of her, and as Jane got paler, and whiter and whiter, the parody of the vampire thing ... And I think that, in this, Meg was meant to be her too in a way, so there was always in Jane's mind ...

Moira Monteith: So, you would see double doubles?

Emma Tennant: They were all doubles. Even the man's name in *The Bad Sister*, Dalzell, is pronounced in Scotland de'il – there isn't one thing in that book which isn't a double.

Sue Roe: To me, each woman was extremely integral and separate. And the notion that they would beware of one another, was totally ...

Emma Tennant: When I worked it out, I remember thinking... I wrote a little list. I put Minnie needs to beware of Fran. They needed to beware of each other, whether they did or not. My view of the book, and I suppose of life still in general, is that men divide and rule. That is to do with separating women, keeping them apart from each other, while all loving him. So the point was, that everybody, of course, was in love with Hugo, and were therefore unable to feel any kind of companionship or friendship with each other.

Sue Roe: Actually that was the other change in *Woman Beware Woman*, because it's the first time that the man is very central in your work. The whole thing is organised around the myth of Hugo. It's not the dead body they are actually dealing with. It's a myth.

Emma Tennant: They all connect through him, in fact, in *Woman Beware Woman* he's like a fuse box.

Moira Monteith: Isn't that the problem with colonialism though? That the people who are subjected must always interlink with those who are dominant and not with each other?

Emma Tennant: Yes. I think it is.

Moira Monteith: Would you see women in that position?

Emma Tennant: I think it would be extraordinary not to.

Sue Roe: I think the title's very successful because it works on such a range of levels. It's got a mirror-image, but with something obstructing. It's the two women, but with a word between instead of a mirror. I read through the book very painstakingly, trying to work out what the problem was. I mean, what Hugo was being accused of having done. And I grappled with a confusion between something political, on a quite large scale – the things he wrote about, the capitalism versus communism – and something very personal. In the end, I decided that was the whole point, that there was that confusion.

Emma Tennant: I think you are absolutely right, in fact. Confusion is very difficult for women who are not involved in any kind of political activity themselves, to come to terms with, because they are looking at the behaviour and beliefs ... obviously my book was very much dictated by having spent some years with the New Left. And finding that this particular combination of very high principled socialist ideas and then the treatment of women which went with it, which of course is, by now old hat, everybody's written about that. I wanted to try and do that fictionally, as far as possible.

Moira Monteith: How do you feel you've used previous writers,

135

	which as far as I can see for both of you in most cases are male writers?
Sue Roe:	Not for me.
Moira Monteith:	Well, Dickens.
Sue Roe:	Yes, but that was accidental. It could have been anybody who wrote about Miss Havisham.
Moira Monteith:	It couldn't have been anybody.
Emma Tennant:	It was Dickens though.
Moira Monteith:	Anybody who reads your book and sees your title, must think 'Dickens'.
Sue Roe:	Fair enough. I started with Estella's name because I loved the name, and also with expectations as a feminist issue. You know, the strain between your romantic and your intellectual expectations. And then I thought, that does link with that very powerful image of those two women by themselves, just by themselves, without any men, in arrested time.
Emma Tennant:	And you were talking earlier about women's voices on their own.
Sue Roe:	I'm finding the novel I'm writing at the moment very difficult, because I know what I want to do, but I can't seem to find a voice as I did when I was writing *Estella* when I heard a kind of chanting in my head. The notion that that kind of chant is totally disassociated from ideas is strange, because I think that finding a voice is to do with identifying an idea. But they *seem* to come disassociated from one another.
Emma Tennant:	So you think the two women in *Estella*, the chant has produced them? Or they belong to the chant, in some way?
Sue Roe:	But the chant couldn't have arisen without the ideas, or vice versa, they split themselves up over time, and come to you separately but actually, the two things are working together.
Moira Monteith:	Would you see them as doubles at all?
Sue Roe:	No. I see Miss Havisham as a kind of mentor. And her appearance is terribly important.

She's the bride, put on ice.

Emma Tennant: Right, it made me think of an Oldenburg sculpture, in your book.

Sue Roe: She's a person made into art, exactly. She's not like a real person any more. She's the images, the stereotypes, and the accessories, frozen, and masquerading as a real person. That's what interested me, that notion of masquerade. That's a very important notion for me.

Emma Tennant: About influences. I would have thought, Colette, and I felt Gustave Moreau who I know wasn't a writer, he was a painter, but it's very painterly your writing. What influences do you think?

Sue Roe: Colette definitely. I read all of Colette, all in French. And, at that time, I was fascinated by Impressionist painting, though I knew nothing about it. One of the things I did when I was in Geneva was to have painting lessons – I was taught by a Frenchman. I was just interested in texture and structure and light. But the other people who have influenced me, really have been Virginia Woolf, very much, and Jean Rhys. Because, I think, both of them have been interested in this notion of getting out of the mainstream, somehow. And, I do think that Virginia Woolf's getting back into the mainstream creates tremendous strain and tremendous ambivalence.

Emma Tennant: What do you mean by 'getting back into the mainstream' in that way?

Sue Roe: Justifying your feminist arguments, in terms of . . . well *Three Guineas* for example: the only way in which she can possibly argue for a strategic feminism is by arguing that all women are outsiders, and that we ought to get together, and instead of presenting a united front, disperse, go off on our own, and be eccentric and drop leaflets down basements, and hope that servants catch them. It's utterly eccentric, as a strategy, and really focuses the strain between her idea of herself as working in isolation and a constraint to define terms.

Emma Tennant: I've just read, in the *London Review of Books*, the most extraordinary attack on Virginia Woolf by John Bayley.

Sue Roe: He likes *The Voyage Out*, doesn't he? He doesn't like all the rest of her work.

Emma Tennant: In this thing he describes her as 'super child'. Again, it's obvious to attack women for being childlike but it seems to me rather unfair.

Sue Roe: She was terribly childlike. She played on her own deepest needs.

Emma Tennant: What writers don't?

Sue Roe: There's nothing as childlike as writing fiction, is there? But there's something . . ., she's doing somehow the same thing as you, but without knowing it, in the sense that she's trying to pull out, another story, after this convergence of history and myth and social –

Emma Tennant: Social observations, yes.

Sue Roe: There's always another story in Virginia Woolf. In any of the novels, there's another story fighting to surface.

Emma Tennant: What would be trying to surface in *To The Lighthouse*? Or what would occur to you?

Sue Roe: The story of the Rayleys, as Lily's attempt to come to terms with Mrs Ramsay's influence over her. I think that one of the main things Lily's trying to do is to come to terms with the immense sexual, maternal, every kind of power of Mrs Ramsay. And I think one of the interesting things is the fact that she deals with this, by making up a story about the Rayleys. And the new story enables her to see husbands and wives and that whole fiction of being married in another perspective.

Moira Monteith: Doesn't that happen in all novels? Isn't there always some subtext pushing forward?

Sue Roe:	I think it does. The interesting thing about Virginia Woolf is that she's subject to this process, she isn't actually in control of it, it happens in spite of her. Whereas, I think in your writing it's one of the things you're actually playing about with.
Emma Tennant:	Not that I'm aware. But, writers do put in subtexts, I suppose, and are aware of them.
Moira Monteith:	I was trying to ask about your – predilection perhaps – for choosing books that seem to me to feed on previous texts. Not so much influences. I don't think for example you can deny that the actual framework of having Dickens there before, must have some impact on anybody who reads.
Sue Roe:	I think it must, but I can't feel responsible for that.
Moira Monteith:	I don't feel you should, but it's there.
Sue Roe:	Right. But from my point of view, I was working, not at all with a fiction, not at all with a story, but with a single image. Just one image.
Emma Tennant:	I think what Moira was saying – when you call something, rather like *Queen of Stones* is obviously *Lord of the Flies*, and this kind of thing, you are asking people to look at a thing in a certain sort of way.
Sue Roe:	Or, if you forget something. I mean, one point about Estella's expectations is that they can't function at all on the same level, or in the same sense, as Pip's. They're nothing to do with earning enough money and being high enough in the social stratum. They're romantic and sexual and they're not to do with ...
Emma Tennant:	But without Pip's they wouldn't exist.
Sue Roe:	Do you think not?
Emma Tennant:	I think the book would exist. You could have called it something else, but I do think that one tricks oneself as a writer, in the most extraordinary way. And it's one long, sort of dis-

139

honesty, and lie, quite honestly. When one says, 'Well, I just did such and such.' And really, the most childlike part is saying that. Because you don't really know whether you would have done it if it had not been for the existence of Pip. One has to think would I have done something like *Queen of Stones* had there not been a great tradition of *Coral Island*, apart from *Lord of the Flies*? No, I shouldn't think so. But mine was much more selfconsciously done than yours. You very often, sometimes that is, base a character on someone, and by the time you've written it, you've completely forgotten who it was originally based on. They take deathless offence and you say, 'How dare you, it was absolutely nothing to do with you at all,' and it had, actually, at some point.

Sue Roe: It had, at the beginning. In that very crucial moment.

Emma Tennant: At some moment it did, and you thought, you saw an angle of their face, in a room, at some time or another and you used them. And they pick it up and are annoyed.

Sue Roe: Well, they'd be justified, because what you actually picked on, even though you might not remember having done so consciously, is the essential thing.

Emma Tennant: Yes, and it can be hurtful of course, if it's something they don't like.

Moira Monteith: Why do you pick male writers, where somebody like Jean Rhys chose a female writer? Though she has disclaimed in her later letters a strong link with Charlotte Brontë, nevertheless I think most readers would see a link. Do you consider yourself re-writing text?

Emma Tennant: Yes. Jean Rhys of course wasn't re-writing, she was pulling out, as with *Estella*, she was pulling out, wasn't she, the first Mrs Rochester?

Sue Roe: Obviously she thought there was an aspect

	that hadn't been dealt with. Re-writing is different from supplying another angle.
Emma Tennant:	Well, there's either supplying another angle, or being inspired by, as I felt I was with *The Bad Sister* certainly.
Moira Monteith:	But I think you're always re-writing. I don't see that it is necessarily reductive.
Emma Tennant:	No. One of the most modish expressions to have somehow crept in when people talk about writing or art at all, is, 'Is she original?' and it's absolutely meaningless. It's like saying somebody isn't relevant.
Sue Roe:	The more I read, the more I want to go on writing.
Emma Tennant:	While you're writing?
Sue Roe:	Yes, actually while.
Emma Tennant:	Only if I was well into something. Once I was about to start something and I happened to be somewhere in the country and picked up a Flannery O'Connor paperback and then, starting something and for five days, Flannery O'Connor pastiche came out. It wasted five days, quite a long time, but it was a throw off and then you have to sort of shut up for three or four weeks, while you start to think, 'Who am I, what voice am I using?' Actually four days ago, I picked up *1984* because I felt that my heroine, in the new book, was entirely speaking in double-think, and I thought, I'm going to explain this novel by saying, 'This is the first ever novel written in double-think.' And then I couldn't write for two days because of Orwell's measured tones, interrupting the ...
Sue Roe:	It's the rhythm that you pick up, isn't it?
Moira Monteith:	So what do you do? Do you have to read things which you feel are quite alien to your own books?
Emma Tennant:	I wouldn't read at all.
Sue Roe:	You don't read.

Moira Monteith: While you're writing?

Emma Tennant: Quite. Except a newspaper or something like that, or unless it's so far gone that nothing's going to stop it.

Sue Roe: But what if a book's going to take five years to write? I mean, what if your life is so structured that you're only going to have intermittent bits of time?

Emma Tennant: I could never have a life like that. I mean, I couldn't do it. If I was told that I had half an hour a day between six and six-thirty, I wouldn't take it, because even at work, I'd write it on my legs or something. In fact, once I started, nothing on earth would stop it. And my books are much too short and I think are done too fast. I sometimes wonder if I didn't have domestic responsibilities whether I would sit down and spend two years on a novel. But I think the answer is that one wouldn't anyway.

Sue Roe: I think I'd write a lot more if I had a lot more time.

Emma Tennant: I would read if I was editing something, because, like you, I like doing something like that as well. Then I can perfectly easily read something that somebody's sent me from the point of view of having advice or doing some editing. What I can't really do is pick up a novel.

Sue Roe: It's the difference between something in progress and something finished.

Emma Tennant: Yes, it probably is. And you can talk to somebody and feel stimulated, exactly, by talking with them.

Moira Monteith: How do you come upon the texts though, that do seem to have fused in your work? For example, why *Lord of the Flies*?

Emma Tennant: I suppose I must put girls reaching the age of puberty in an extreme situation, because I want to examine myths and or lies or both, about puberty. So, really, what better, and then people said, it's this *Picnic at Hanging Rock* or something. There have been many, many in the genre. I think it's then better to say that's what you're doing and make overt references to it. But on the whole, whenever I write anything, I do my reading and research before starting.

Sue Roe: It was the notion that having brought together all these possible interpretations and possible stories, and different ways of piecing together this mysterious thing that happened, still nobody quite knew why; nobody could quite explain the ultimate impulses. Then there was a basis for the reader to put together his or her own interpretation.

Emma Tennant: Quite. That's what I hoped. A friend said she thought I put too much of Freud's Dora into the book. But I did that precisely as a slight joke, that psychoanalysts would then think 'Oh, this is the Dora case'. But I think that a lot of people didn't get that sort of tongue-in-cheek –

Sue Roe: It's a pity, because it was pure parody wasn't it?

Emma Tennant: Good, I'm glad you saw that. Some people didn't at all.

Sue Roe: The housewife with the linen cupboard, for example, was very funny actually, it was very witty.

Emma Tennant: I was actually asked to write a script of that for Channel 4 and I couldn't get it right. They asked me to do it twice and a third time and I thought I couldn't afford actually to go on re-writing. I'm obviously not very good at scripts. The person there, a very nice man called Walter Donahue, and I were talking about it and he said, 'It's about two queens coming out of a closet.' Mary, Queen of Scots and Queen Elizabeth are actually kissing in a linen cupboard. They were obviously having a sort of

143

lesbian kiss. So I thought, 'Is that in some extraordinary way what inspired this? But of course, it wasn't. It's just people say things like that, which make you think, 'God, is that what I was really writing about, queens coming out of a closet?'

Moira Monteith: But it did seem to me, when I read it, that the book would not have come into existence if it had not been for *Lord of the Flies*. I mean you would have written a different book, if you hadn't read that. So why did that have so much influence?

Sue Roe: Did you read that at a formative time in your life?

Emma Tennant: Actually I was one of those lucky people who was spared it at school. My daughter, my elder one, is now writing essays on Piggy. No, as I say, I never liked it, but I was interested in the genre of the extreme situation, the island or whatever, which is a science fiction device, isn't it? And you might as well take that, and slightly make the point that boys being together will lead to a certain sort of mutual destructiveness and so on; and girls being brought together in that kind of way will lead to some unpleasant kind of rivalry which is very different from boys being brought together. I suppose that was the point.

Sue Roe: And you were talking very much about class, weren't you? Because I'm always shocked, when I read *Queen of Stones* that it had to be Melanie who was ultimately the victim.

Emma Tennant: I suppose again, there may be a Piggy sort of thing there. But I thought it was very important. It is shocking, but I felt it was likely.

Sue Roe: Because she has the least power in the group? She's the least articulate really.

Emma Tennant: She's the least articulate. She's had a rotten time. The others are, without knowing it, already brought up in such a way by their

middle-class or upper-class backgrounds to
hate her. I'm afraid it's a horrible message but
they are.

Sue Roe: It's not only that, it's physical. She's ugly.
Emma Tennant: She's ugly, absolutely.
Moira Monteith: She's dependent, in fact?
Emma Tennant: Yes. And so they're going to – when it really
comes down to it – turn against her, rather
than each other.
Sue Roe: And there's that wonderful moment where she
constructs the possibility of having been
changed with Jane in the cradle. The first time
I read it, I actually believed that. I thought,
'Ah, here's a twist in the plot.' It was completely credible in the context of your work. And
then, in retrospect you see that this is Melanie
constructing her own fiction.
Emma Tennant: Apparently that is one of the deepest stories.
I think I probably read it in Bettelheim, but
I've often read it. This enormous man striding
across the sky, with the baby tucked in the
arms, having done the swap. And as children
are obviously so uncertain about who they are,
the thing of being swapped, is only too possible, isn't it?
Sue Roe: Were you uncertain about who you were?
I wasn't at all uncertain about who I was. Not
that I knew who I was. It just wasn't a question
I asked myself.
Emma Tennant: I'd no idea who I was. My parents were away
in the war. My father was in the SOE. I was
completely alone in this valley.
Sue Roe: And you were aware of not having any idea?
Emma Tennant: Oh no, you can't be, when you're very young.
But what I'm aware of is the nursery rhyme,
that used to make me scream and scream at
$2\frac{1}{2}$, about the old woman who went to market,
and on the way back she fell asleep by the side
of the road and some little boy comes and cuts
her petticoat off to the knee. And she wakes up

and shouts, 'This is none of me.' And apparently the screams just went up the valley and down, I was so upset. You don't know who you are, you're changing into somebody else, or whatever. You've woken up and you're somebody else, it's the most frightening thing of course that can possibly happen. So I think all people can do when they look at their early childhood is to try and see what frightens them or what excited them and then they'll find out.

Sue Roe: And do you use what frightened you, in your fiction?

Emma Tennant: I suppose so. Yes, I use it to frighten other people.

Sue Roe: Do you do the same for images?

Emma Tennant: In one book called *Alice Fell* I did actually put the woman, having her skirts cut up to the knee but that was a sort of poetic effort. Yes, I suppose there are images which are absolutely terrifying to me.

Sue Roe: And that's the problem. They continue to be so, even though you've dealt with them or placed them.

Emma Tennant: Oh much less. I'm one of those stupid people who actually believes that writing makes me better. I can't stop myself from writing, but when I get things like that, when I express them, and I feel I've been able to do so in some kind of artistic way, I feel tremendously pleased and satisfied and freed of them. So although it's the fashion now, to say it makes no difference at all, and that you must have endless psychoanalysis or whatever, and that people are neurotics and they stay neurotics whether they write or paint or not, I don't believe it's true. I think that for certain people to be prevented – I think that Tillie Olsen is a brilliant example. I mean both *Silences* and *Tell me a Riddle* are the best descriptions there's ever been of creative people being clamped down by poverty and domestic horror, and going almost into a zone of complete madness.

Moira Monteith: Why do you think you didn't write until you were thirty-four?

Emma Tennant: Oh, I did.

Moira Monteith: Yes, I know you said that. But you published only one book.

Emma Tennant: My confidence was killed by what happened to that book. I wrote three 400-page novels between that and *The Crack*.

Moira Monteith: Tillie Olsen's point is specifically about the different publishing careers of women and middle-class men, isn't it?

Emma Tennant: Oh yes.

Moira Monteith: Would you feel that that is appropriate to you at all?

Emma Tennant: I think that to come from the background I come from and to be taken seriously, not to be humiliated by jokes about your privileged background, I think it's not as difficult or as horrible, because there's nothing as difficult and as horrible, no doubt – I don't know that I really mean this – than to come from a Tillie Olsen kind of background. But if you look at my background and you look at who has come as a serious writer out of it, and Nancy Mitford for instance is a good writer, but she went off very quickly into doing historical novels. I don't think that Vita Sackville West was much good. You name to me somebody who's actually taken seriously, isn't thought to be a bit of a laugh who comes from my background. It's a very difficult thing to fight against. Confidence can be removed at once.

Sue Roe: Are you talking about landscape or class?

Emma Tennant: Class.

Sue Roe: Caroline Blackwood?

Emma Tennant: Caroline Blackwood is taken seriously. She's about the only other person. She's a very serious writer and an extraordinary person.

147

Sue Roe: What about that gap between suffering from the horror of the things that were frightening, and turning them into fiction. Did you never resist turning what was frightening into what could become acceptable, isn't that process of turning something scary into fiction and making it all right, something one resists?

Emma Tennant: You only resist it if you don't know how to do it. Which is why I think you have to learn so much about technique, and that is the thing that I really object to, not being taught in schools. One day, when I have more time, I would hope to be able to go round schools. The point is, you sit there, you do all these lessons, you read *Julius Caesar*, you fall fast asleep. You have to analyse Piggy, but no one actually tells you how to write and there are certain tips. If you have no – whatever it is that makes you write – then you won't write anyway. It took me years to learn them. I was taught them by the science fiction writers.

Moira Monteith: You said in the interview with John Haffenden that you took the science fiction writers as a signpost, a structure, not the theme.

Emma Tennant: The theme, that you could never teach. Because a theme must come from some extraordinary thing in the person. But what's not taught is not only a question of structure but tense. I mean, how you can move several times if you want in one sentence between tenses, and rather enliven things. How you can break from one subject to another. It takes a long time to learn a few simple things because of having to work them out oneself and thinking, 'What's wrong with this thing, why is it so funny on the page?'

Sue Roe: It goes back to this question of voice and chanting. The whole impulse of creative writing sometimes is the impulse to break the rules, to let the rhythms of what's actually pushing you towards expressing a thing in writing, take over on the page.

Emma Tennant: But then I think you have to be very careful that it doesn't take over entirely. I felt with your book, of your being a poet, that for you to continue writing, this isn't just me being bossy, twenty years older etc., but to continue writing novels, you would need to make sure it didn't happen too much, to control it, and cut and paragraph more. You're writing apropos, which I think is a marvellous thing to be able to do, and you're an absolutely natural, poetic writer.

Sue Roe: I think you have to make a break between narrative and poetry, I agree and that's what I'm trying to do at the moment. It's terribly difficult. You can't just make a technical break, all the other things are called into question. I mean in order to make a technical break from *Estella* I need to stop writing in such short, breathless sentences as I did before, and stop making it so very synaesthetic. But then you have to have a different thing to write about, have to be moved by a different set of circumstances, to have a different sense of timing. And one of the things I'm struggling with at the moment is the attempt to channel the force – for me – of the material into a sequence of events, which I think is very powerfully effected in *Woman Beware Woman*. The sequence of events actually, I felt, influenced the style of writing in that novel.

Emma Tennant: You see *Colomba* did supply that, the sequence of events, leading to this accidental, on-purpose revenge killing. It is wonderfully useful to be given something of that sort, on a plate, or to choose it.

Moira Monteith: You have said that plotting is very important in most of your books.

Emma Tennant: Yes, I think so. Some of my books lack narrative because they're meant to. Bruno Schultz influenced *Wild Nights* and if anyone reads his *Street of Crocodiles*, it's much better than *Wild Nights*, but there's no plot. The plot is the seasons and the weather.

Sue Roe: And the wind changes?

Emma Tennant: And the wind changes. The psychological thing of the people there being the climate.

Sue Roe: It's much more biological too. It goes in cycles rather than from beginning to end.

Emma Tennant: It's got a full year in it, I think. One of the problems for me is that I've written too many different sorts of books. There are three sorts of comic science fictions. And then there are the sort of 'woman' ones, if you like, *The Bad Sister*, *Queen of Stones*, *Woman Beware Woman*, and then the poetic ones. So that there doesn't seem to be much coherence, and I think it's quite difficult to be like that.

Sue Roe: Because you need to have an identity? And a function as a novelist?

Moira Monteith: Is there a pressure then, when you begin a new novel, to write in the way you've written previously?

Emma Tennant: Pressure from outside? No, I don't think so.

Sue Roe: I don't think there is.

Moira Monteith: So where does the problem lie? That you can't be identified as a science fiction writer or whatever?

Emma Tennant: That's right. I think that, although I don't make my whole career being a novelist and get these editing jobs, I would obviously prefer to do less of editing and be able to make more as a writer. It's as simple as that.

Sue Roe: I think I'd rather have to struggle along doing different kinds of jobs if this somehow encourages changes in the writing than only write in one way, wouldn't you?

Emma Tennant: I don't know. I suppose what every writer would like more than anything, would be to write one absolutely extraordinary book, which everyone wanted to read. Rather like *Empire of the Sun* by Jimmy Ballard. To write a book in which all his earlier images, which were thought to be totally imaginative, turn out to have belonged to his childhood. It is wonderful to come full circle ...

Sue Roe: And have some sense of authority?

Emma Tennant: Probably a lot of writers must rather hope, to get to a stage where they see all the images and all the ideas and themes they've had earlier on, which have all been apparently disparate, and do belong to some early part of life as everything must, in some way gathered together, and then come out in some magnificent book which is both serious and popular. That must have been what Dickens actually had, all the time.

Sue Roe: I think my greatest ambition is to feel that I've said it. Whatever it was I wanted to say, just to feel that it's actually said.

Emma Tennant: Apparently no one's ever felt that. Writers on their deathbed say, 'I wish I'd said it.'

Sue Roe: I'm not surprised.

Moira Monteith: Emma, you have said that, certainly *Queen of Stones*, if not other books were didactic and you're both talking as if you actually have a message. So you must have a reader that you conceive as receiving that message?

Emma Tennant: You can be didactic in some books, of course, and not in others. But on the whole, you write the book and it wasn't what you meant to say.

Sue Roe: That's right.

Moira Monteith: But you must say it to somebody mustn't you?

Sue Roe: No, not necessarily.

Moira Monteith: Well, how could you just say something?

Sue Roe: Because you do have a sense of an audience. I mean like when you're playing the piano, and your music teacher says, 'Imagine they are cabbages' so that you don't have a nervous

151

breakdown on the stage. You just look down,
and that is the audience. There's not a person
whose mind you know what's going on in. You
don't have a sense of a receptive mind, that
somebody out there understands what ...
I mean it's not quite as precise as that, is
it? You don't have a sense of a *particular*
audience.

Emma Tennant: Only when you are aware that you're doing
something didactic; then it's possible to answer and say, 'I see somebody, two or three
years older than my daughter is now', sort of
thing. Otherwise I agree with you. I've no idea
who on earth you think you write for.

Sue Roe: Do you have response blocks, in the way that
Mrs Houghton has writing blocks? Not just
when you sit at the desk with your piece of
paper and your pencil, but times in which you
feel you can't respond to anything that's going
on, and you'll never turn anything that's going
on, into writing.

Emma Tennant: Yes. Also I think it's very miserable, I'm sure
it's true for most writers, when you've finished
something, and say the publisher likes it, and it
comes out and even some reviewers like it,
you're dead to it. You can't on the whole enjoy
the fruits of your, probably pointless efforts. It
seems very sad, all that. Very common. A kind
of staleness. I think the definition of hell would
be to sit on an island with nothing but your
own work.

Moira Monteith: Virginia Woolf, if you go by her diary, always
felt particularly depressed once her book was
out, didn't she?

Emma Tennant: Yes.

Sue Roe: She also had the thought that she hadn't quite
said it, partly because I don't think she ever
knew quite what it was she wanted to say. I
think that sometimes she kidded herself quite
effectively, and then having published it, rea-

lised that that wasn't it at all. I really don't think she ever did know quite what it was she wanted to say. I think we can know, but I don't think she did.

Moira Monteith: Do you have a sense of yourselves as authors? A particular authorial voice?

Emma Tennant: Do you?

Sue Roe: I have a secret sense of myself as an author and it doesn't matter yet if nobody else recognizes it because I've only written one novel and one kind of novel. But ultimately, I think the only way you can go on is to believe that in the end, writing is what you're here for. Because it's got to override everything else. It's got to happen on a different level, don't you think? Because otherwise you just simply wouldn't be able to do it. It's not simply a way of amalgamating your thoughts and getting them down, it's some other, it's some more powerful ...

Emma Tennant: Yes. I actually think that there are certain patterns which certain people seem to carry in them, which something has got to conform to. In my case, there seems to be always a left and a right, a double kind of a thing and a circle in some way. I think, in most writers, there's some sort of pattern. And they'll find that the book will try and force itself to follow the pattern that belongs to the author.

7

THE OPEN CAGE: FREEDOM, MARRIAGE AND THE HEROINE IN EARLY TWENTIETH-CENTURY AMERICAN WOMEN'S NOVELS

Shirley Foster

Recent feminist criticism has illuminatingly revealed how female writers, subject to pressures unknown to their male counterparts, are forced to find indirect means of questioning their society's orthodoxies in their work. As such criticism has indicated, artistic as well as social ideologies have prevented women novelists in particular from articulating openly their own dissent from accepted notions of female roles, especially those concerning the sacredness of marriage and motherhood; in order to formulate their protest, they have had to implement strategies of deviousness, using artistic devices which voice their unease without obviously challenging literary or sexual conventions. At the same time, their awareness of the complex and often contradictory nature of female aspiration produces ambiguities or dualities in their writing, a reflection of ambivalence as much as of outrage. The problem of how to convey a personal vision of womanhood in their art without violating current codes was especially acute for nineteenth-century women novelists, confronted with powerful images of 'normality' in both social and literary spheres (the domestic angel must herself provide her novel with a happy matrimonial conclusion), but it has continued to exercise twentieth-century writers, who are still exploring ways of expressing their resistance to restrictive and falsifying ideologies about womanhood.

In order to examine more closely the ways in which accomplished female novelists can incorporate both protest and ambivalence into a traditional form, I have chosen three novels – Kate Chopin's *The Awakening* (1899), Edith Wharton's *The House of Mirth* (1905) and Willa Cather's *The Song of the Lark* (first version, 1915) – whose authors, linked in time and subject-matter and themselves representing deviation from the standard feminine ideal, use their work to articulate their sense of the destructiveness of conventions which condemn women to a single function. In each case, they embody their dissent in certain images and themes, their contrasting treatment of which reveals how, as female writers, they not only share feelings of dissatisfaction but also draw on similar material in order to express these feelings. Chopin, Wharton and Cather are all writing in a period of transition in terms of the 'woman question'. Legislative reform in America had begun to improve conditions for their sex: there had been various Married Women's Property Acts by the end of the nineteenth century, and by the second decade of the twentieth most states had conceded the female vote, for example. It was therefore theoretically easier for women to dissent openly from restricting definitions of sexual function than it had been for their mothers and grandmothers. Traditionalism, however, still wielded considerable power in a country highly concerned with establishing and maintaining moral and social stability. Moreover, early twentieth-century American feminists, as much as their nineteenth-century predecessors, retained an essentially conservative view of female characteristics and roles, clinging to the belief that marriage and maternity must remain as the basis of all female influence. Jane Addams, for instance, who was radical enough to demand independence for the unmarried woman, did not challenge the orthodox 'placing' of women in the home, the centre from which all change must be generated, while vigorous protestors such as Emma Goldman and Ellen Key not only supported the continuance of the man/woman unit but actually accorded motherhood an almost sacred status.[1] Against this background of dualistic thought about womanhood, these three novelists explore the possibilities of defining female individuality in terms other than sexual relativity. While each challenges the power of conventional images, she is herself ultimately ambivalent about women's needs and goals. The artistic patterns in their work thus voice both their awareness of the paradoxes of their sex's position and their own questionings.

It is best to begin discussion with *The House of Mirth*, Wharton's second and perhaps best-known novel, because although it is not the earliest of the three works, it is most clearly the fruit of a dualistic outlook. Wharton herself both adhered to the orthodoxies of her convention-ridden background, whose values she could, or would not wholly reject, and energetically espoused the new age of dissenting and more adventurous womanhood. Her fictional treatment of female roles is shaped by the tensions which she experienced as the highly-intelligent product of an ordered, unimaginative and enclosed world of old New York families, which considered marriage axiomatic for women and had no place for female literary or artistic propensities. Her criticism of her own society is sharpened by her awareness of her conflicting roles as wife-cum-hostess, enacting and to a considerable extent enjoying the mores of her social circle, and as a writer seeking the enrichment of cultural contact and liberation from the anti-intellectualism of her own sphere. Wharton's depiction of her heroine's situation in *The House of Mirth* is also coloured by her interest in deterministic environmental theories, which she encountered in the late 1880s when she was introduced by her friend Egerton Winthrop to the works of Darwin, Spencer, Huxley and Haeckel. Her reading strengthened her belief that human beings are moulded and trapped by external conditions, a view which the position of the woman of her day seemed particularly to confirm.[2] Her protest against the tyranny of matrimonial creeds is thus characterised by an ironic control combined with an almost fatalistic perception, rather than by passionate outrage; and she directs her attention not to possible alternative modes of female fulfilment but to revealing how matrimony, now stripped of its romantic embellishments, has become a material transaction, the predominant element in women's fight for survival.

Marriage in *The House of Mirth*, whose title ironically underlines Wharton's recognition of the hypocrisies of her world, is an institution built on greed concealing itself as respectability, and functioning on bitterness, jealousy or mere indifference; beneath its precariously maintained surface betrayal and intrigue are rife.

The heroine, Lily Bart, is intelligent enough to recognise this, but she is unable to defy the dictatorship of the society which has created her. Brought up to believe that money is essential to personal satisfaction, she sees that success is dependent upon a union which will combine material gratification and social status; romantic emotion is an indulgence she cannot afford. Taught that her beauty, her only asset, must be exploited to the full, Lily almost automatically responds to her inherited desires, themselves the creation of her environment. Early in the novel, Lawrence Selden, the one man of her acquaintance who appears to have successfully evaded society's domination, says to her, 'Isn't marriage your vocation? Isn't it what you've all been brought up for?', and her dispirited reply, 'I suppose so. What else is there?'[3] indicates her astute but helpless acknowledgement that she is a victim of her own civilisation. Selden sees the links of her bracelet as 'manacles chaining her to her fate' (p. 8), an insight echoed by Lily herself when she admits to her cousin, Gerty Farish, that 'the beginning was in my cradle, I suppose – in the way I was brought up, and the things I was taught to care for' (p. 261).

Wharton makes it clear that, for all her awareness, Lily has no viable alternatives open to her. A single, self-supporting existence, symbolised by Gerty's 'mediocre and ... ineffectual' (p. 103) life-style, with its round of small philanthropies, scanty meals, and 'mean and shabby surroundings' – all the 'squalid compromises of poverty' (p. 30) – is inconceivable to Lily, who wants at least a glamorous imprisonment. Wharton presents Gerty's miserable spinsterhood as not only unattractive but distasteful; in a rare authorial interpolation, she reduces her to insect-like dimensions: 'Gerty had always been a parasite in the moral order, living on the crumbs of other tables, and content to look through the window at the banquet spread for her friends' (p. 174). She also sees no hope in women trying to maintain economic independence, as is clear from Lily's dismal failure at the millinery establishment. Even if Wharton is guilty here of misrepresentation (obviously some women of her generation were able to support themselves), Lily's experience aptly reinforces the idea of her victimisation by a ruthless society. The only other possible alternative for her is marriage based on wholly different premises, and, quite apart from the fact that Selden's moral shabbiness diminishes his husbandly potential, Lily's conditioning prevents her from considering seriously this option either – love without money is no better than independence without money. Unlike the central characters in the other two novels, who positively resist or rebel against the chains of matrimony, Lily seems to have no real choice in the matter. Not only is she temperamentally unable to cut herself off from the society which is destroying her and develop an independent selfhood, but she encounters an almost Hardyesque fatality of events whenever she attempts to step outside her predetermined role, such as when she meets Sim Rosedale after leaving Selden's apartment.

Without directly articulating her criticism, Wharton conveys her sense of the powerlessness of women against such social tyranny by using conventional imagery in an unconventional way, thus at once indicating her heroine's predicament and uncovering the false ideologies which control her. Certain key images referring to women recur in all three novels; in Wharton's case, she deliberately inverts the traditional meanings attached to them, so that metaphors for female aspiration or fulfilment which we find in Chopin and Cather in her hands become symbols of restriction. Foremost are her images drawn from nature, appropriate to her naturalistic and deterministic mode of thought. Lily's beauty, her sole means of matrimonial negotiation, is that of all graceful living things, but, like them, she is ultimately dependent for survival on her environment, not on her individual qualities. Biologically as well as socially conditioned, she is 'like a water-plant' carried hither and thither by 'the flux of the tides' (p. 62). Her attractiveness, unwilled by her, becomes the agent of its own destruction:

> Inherited tendencies had combined with early training to make her the highly specialized product she was: an organism as helpless out of its narrow range as the sea-anemone torn from the rock. She had been fashioned to adorn and delight; to what other end does nature round the rose-leaf and paint the humming-bird's breast? And was it her fault that the purely decorative mission is less easily and harmoniously fulfilled among social beings than in the world of nature? (p. 350)

Lily's brief lapses into 'natural' behaviour also always prove disastrous in terms of her social goals; again, nature is shown as ultimately treacherous, both controlling the individual and increasing her vulnerability in the sphere in which she has been placed. One of the few scenes in the novel which take place outdoors is that in which Selden and Lily discuss the possibility of her 'freedom' – a discussion itself made feasible only because Lily has impulsively abandoned her pursuit of the rich, dull, but eligible Percy Gryce in favour of a walk with Selden. As Wharton's recent biographer has shown, she often uses images of interiors in her fiction to express women's entrapment;[4] here, the open country, belying its external charms, forges one more link in the chain which encircles Lily. The golden autumn day, which to Lily seems 'the accomplice of her mood ... a day for impulse and truancy' (p. 67), betrays her by luring her – with fatal consequences, it transpires – away from her only possible strategy of survival. In such a setting, she feels her 'free spirit' expanding beyond her 'little black prisonhouse of fears' (p. 75), but the idea of freedom is to prove as ephemeral as the peace and beauty of the natural surroundings, broken when Gryce's insect-like car hums into view to remind Lily of the inexorable conditions of her present existence. Furthermore, with brilliant irony, Wharton has Selden propound his theory of 'personal freedom ... a republic of the spirit' (p. 79), against this apparently idyllic background; the pastoral perfection of the scene mockingly glosses the delusiveness of this theory, as well as Selden's own essential cowardice and unreliability. When, later, Lily is again momentarily drawn by the possibilities of love and freedom which Selden seems to offer, the natural background now overtly represents deceptiveness. The Brys's garden, in which Selden and Lily briefly come together, is the product of ostentatious wealth and social ambition; hung with lights which make the trees look like caves and give water substantiality, it is a 'magic place' whose 'unreality' is a 'part of their own dream-like sensations' (p. 159).

A similar transformation of meaning occurs with Wharton's use of bird imagery in the novel. Perhaps influenced by James's *The Portrait of a Lady* (1881), in which Isabel Archer, like a wild creature refusing to be tamed, resists being trapped in War-burton's 'system', but is finally imaged by Ralph Touchett as a fallen bird 'caught' and 'put into a cage' when she decides to marry Osmond,[5] Wharton portrays her heroine as a bird whose flight takes her further into the prison she thinks she is escaping. Hopeful of a triumphant marriage, Lily feels herself soaring not to a sphere liberating her from the manacles of civilisation, but to 'that empyrean of security where creditors cannot penetrate' (p. 57); to an extension of her cash-orientated world, in fact. Later, as her exultation fades and her hopes disappear, she realises that it was only 'fancy [which] had fluttered free pinions' (p. 90) and which gave 'wings to all her hopes' (p. 107). And though she knows that the door of the 'great gilt cage', in which, like a captive bird, she is penned, is in theory 'always open' (p. 64), she realises equally well that she cannot will her escape; her natural faculties are powerless against the grim determinism which rules her life.

One other image which Wharton draws on in common with the other two novelists, albeit more peripherally, is that of female creativity. The idea of suppressed womanhood speaking through artistry is found in much nineteenth-century women's literature (with Vashti in *Villette* and the Princess in *Daniel Deronda*, for instance) and it is important in both *The Awakening* and *The Song of the Lark*. In *The House of Mirth*, Wharton once more takes a familiar idea and gives it a different significance. Lily's pose as Reynold's 'Mrs Lloyd' in the Brys's *tableaux vivants* is no expression of female individuality reaching beyond the role which society expects it to play. Though she has wisely relied for effect on her own beauty, momentarily 'detached from all that cheapened and vulgarised it' (p. 157), in using 'her artistic intelligence in selecting a type so like her own that she could embody the person represented without ceasing to be herself' (p. 156), Lily reveals her lack of capacity to transcend the ideal of outward female perfection whose symbol she has become. Unlike Chopin's Edna or Cather's Thea, she is unable to lose her social form in the articulation of a new selfhood; her presentation is a means of meeting the elaborate dissimulation of her world on its own terms. In the same way that nature in this novel is an image of destructiveness, and freedom signifies closer restriction, so here self-expression has become the perfect artefact.

It was suggested earlier that ambivalence as well as protest characterises most women writers' response to prevailing sexual ideologies. As we have seen, Wharton's own experience in particular encouraged an ambivalent outlook. Having achieved the 'normality' of a marriage which was to prove increasingly frustrating and stultifying (after nearly thirty years of being married, she finally obtained a divorce in 1914), she was torn between rejecting the values of her convention-ridden society and participating in the attractions it still held for her. Though she was clearly aware of this personal duality, her novel suffers from an element of ambiguity which gives the effect of evasiveness and which threatens to undermine the cool clarity of her vision as a whole. In the first place, Wharton demands that we regard Lily not just as a victim but as a responsible ethical being, capable of moral choice and dependent upon that capacity for our respect. To some extent this enhances the theme of female helplessness: Lily has a finer sensibility than those around her and is aware of the compromises necessary to gain her ends, but she is too much the slave to circumstances to act out her moral awareness, except in brief high moments such as at the end of the novel when she uses her legacy to pay off the debts incurred to Gus Trenor. But by implying that Lily holds at least some of the threads of her fate in her own hands, Wharton tends to undercut her chilling vision of bound womanhood.

Even more damagingly, there is a vein of sentimentality in the book which blurs its overall clear-sightedness. The depiction of the coldly unromantic nature of sexual relationships in this society effectively heightens the real horror of matrimonial bondage, yet the aura of romance between Lily and Selden hovers over much of the story, and 'love' is the unspoken word between them at the end of the book. Though, as has been pointed out, Selden is far from ideal – Wharton herself called him 'a negative hero'[6] – the final scene, in which Lily, convinced that her feeling for him will never be reciprocated, acknowledges him as her mentor, glosses over his deficiencies. It also relies for its effect on the conventional pathos of unfulfilled female desire and the ideality, if not the actuality, of the traditional romantic conclusion. It is notable, moreover, that Lily's last vision of comfort is the warm family nest symbolised by the working-class girl, Nettie, and her baby – a stereotyped image of womanly satisfaction which, denied Lily, intensifies the sadness of her last hours. There may be deliberate ambiguity here – the sensation of contact with the child lulls Lily into her final, drug-ridden sleep, and, like Cleopatra's asp, 'the tender pressure of its body' (p. 376) at her breast takes her out of life – but if female domesticity embodied in maternity kills, it also confers a final peace. Lily is released from her prison, not as a revolutionary spirit but as a potential wife and mother. An uncertainty of stance, the result of combined adherence to convention and personal ambivalence, unsettles what is other-wise a poised and penetrating denouement of the position of women in a society to whose demands they must conform or else perish.

Although *The Awakening* appeared at the very end of the nineteenth century, in 1899, both thematically and stylistically it strikes as being more 'advanced' than *The House of Mirth*; indeed, according to one account, it is two decades ahead of its time.[7] Its most obvious innovativeness is its depiction of the female attempt to break with stereotypical creeds of woman-hood and find a new, independent self. Its creative boldness, which led to its immediate withdrawal from the St Louis public libraries and cast its author into literary disrepute (she was denied membership of the local fine arts club, and the widespread critical disapprobium probably made her reluctant to write any more), is unmarred by the kind of sentimentality which has been noted in Wharton's work; it also represents a much more positive challenge to sexual orthodoxies than the later novel.

Chopin herself is a more enigmatic figure than Wharton. On the face of it she seems a model of female conventionality. She was brought up in St Louis, within a sphere of established southern mores; she became one of the belles of the city, married at nineteen and had six children, and played an overtly traditional feminine role as Lady Bountiful on her husband's Louisiana plantation. Yet she also clearly longed for a more expansive existence, and the unconventionality which she exhibited as a child, reading extensively and preferring her own company to more communal entertainment, continued into adulthood in desires and aspirations which, concealed beneath the surface of her life, found expression in her fictional themes.

The fact that she did not begin to write until after her husband's death in itself suggests creative talent suppressed by the requirements of matrimony, and the number of her stories which portray women stifled by unsatisfactory marriages implies that she was not so content with her lot as might appear. Though her life-style was not so ostensibly fraught with division as Wharton's, the rebellious spirit of many of her heroines probably enacts her own deep feelings of dissatisfaction with the current restrictiveness of female roles. Like Wharton, she was considerably influenced by Darwinian theory and was convinced that women were especially subject to the immutable laws of nature and biological destiny, but her belief that human beings still had some free choice encouraged her depiction of women positively opposing the traditional activities of their sex and seeking new means of self-expression. Well aware that, for American writers, 'the limitations imposed upon their art by their environment hamper a full and spontaneous expression', she nevertheless wanted to strip off the veil of hypocrisy 'with which ethical and conventional standards have draped [human existence]'[8] – a veil which she knew fell particularly heavily over women.

The heroine of *The Awakening*, Edna Pontellier, has more power to control her own fate than Lily Bart has. Though she is married and must therefore 'find' herself from within an already defined role, Chopin allows her more freedom, both social and cosmic, than Wharton permits Lily. She is not the evident pawn of a hostile fate, nor is she the complete victim of a code-ridden society which destroys the unorthodox; as we shall see, not all the women in her world are entirely conformist. Edna is also beyond the tyranny of the cash nexus which so dominates Lily's life; unthreatened by material deprivation and with the means of indulging her love of beautiful things, she calmly appropriates her husband's income to make her own purchases. Importantly too, she is able to make money for herself by painting. With her greater advantages, Chopin's heroine displays more active opposition than Wharton's to the values of her society. The 'awakening' of the title indicates her growing recognition that the stultification which marriage imposes on the female personality must be resisted. When the novel opens, Edna is for the first time no longer content to be regarded as a piece of property (significantly our initial view of her is through M. Pontellier's eyes, when he sees her as a sunshade coming up the beach) nor to be subject to her husband's whims and insistence on her social conformity. Recognising that her marriage was purely an accidental formality, she begins her protest in actions such as refusing to go into the house after the late evening bathing excursion, almost startled to perceive 'that her will had blazed up, stubborn and resistant'.[9] Later, she takes even more positive steps towards independence: she refuses to undertake the social duty of receiving afternoon calls; she throws off her wedding-ring and tries to destroy it; and she makes the crucial decision to move to a house of her own, rented with her own earnings, instinctively casting off her husband's support, as she has 'apprehended instinctively the dual life – that outward existence which conforms, the inward life which questions' (p. 26).

It is significant also that Edna rejects the conditions which marriage as an institution imposes upon women. Her friend, Mme Ratignolle, whom she sees as the conventional Madonna, a queen with her brood of children, comes to represent a wholly undesirable model; when she goes to dinner with the Ratignolles, Edna is depressed by the chilling negativeness of such a life:

> The little glimpse of domestic harmony which had been offered her, gave her no regret, no longing. It was not a condition of life which fitted her, and she could see in it but an appalling and hopeless ennui. She was moved by a kind of commiseration for Madame Ratignolle – a pity for that colorless existence which never uplifted its possessor beyond the region of blind contentment in which no murmur of anguish ever visited her soul, in which she would never have the taste of life's delirium. (pp. 93-4)

This is far from the image of domestic and maternal bliss which Lily yearns towards at the end of *The House of Mirth*. In this novel, Chopin presents children unequivocally as a source of entrapment. Edna loves her sons, but not obsessively or exclusively. She sees them as a burden of responsibility which must be thrown off if the individual female self is to survive, as her comment to her somewhat shocked friend indicates: 'I would give my money, I would give my life for my children, but

I wouldn't give myself' (p. 80). Childbearing comes to be seen, in fact, as a biological snare, a harsh edict of nature which renders women helpless in an unchosen role; the almost sinister whisper of Mme Ratignolle, exhausted after the birth of yet another child, urging the wayward Edna to 'remember the children' (p. 182) echoes like a death-knell in the younger woman's ears, telling her of the hopelessness of her revolt in the face of Nature's 'decoy to secure mothers for the race' (p. 184).

In *The Awakening*, then, Chopin is both asserting the need for women to free themselves from the bonds of stifling convention and portraying her heroine's progress towards recognition of and rebellion against these bonds. Like Wharton, she conveys her outlook through recurring imagery, much of it drawn from nature or natural functions; her novel, more tightly conceived than Wharton's, is structured on clear metaphorical patterns. Like Wharton, too, she remains ambivalent about the notion of female separateness, particularly as regards its psychological ramifications, but whereas, as we have seen, Wharton's dualistic response produces a sense of unease or evasiveness, Chopin's is intrinsic to her presentation of aspiring womanhood. Thus she uses her images deliberately so as to suggest ambiguity, not simply reversing the familiar signification but conveying a double implication. Edna's aspirations are frequently described in terms of dreams, which, associated with hopefulness and unwilled 'natural' responses, are emblematic of both vision and illusion, each deriving from deep inner desires. Having been stirred by Mlle Reisz's piano-playing to make her daring aquatic venture, Edna later feels that the whole night's experience has been like a dream. Again, after she has challenged her husband's authority, as her exhilaration slowly slips away, she 'began to feel like one who awakens gradually out of a dream ... to feel again the realities pressing into her soul' (p. 53). Her visions of romantic love are also like narcotic-induced dreams, blotting out the less attractive actualities of her present life. And she herself expresses her final disillusionment in similar terms:

> if one might go on sleeping and dreaming – but to wake up and find
> – oh! well! perhaps it is better to wake up after all, even to suffer,
> rather than to remain a dupe to illusions all one's life. (p. 184)

In this way, Chopin shows that a woman's attempt to reject the 'realities' is both a passionate expression of inner selfhood and a self-deceptive idealism; paradoxically, Edna is awakening to a partially delusive enlightenment.

The same duality operates with the bird image which recurs in the novel as a symbol of both aspiration and defeat. Edna is not the traditional mother figure, 'fluttering about with extended, protecting wings' (p. 16). She is instead, as Mlle Reisz tells her, to be a bird of another kind, with 'strong wings' to 'soar above the level plain of tradition and prejudice' (p. 138). But at the end of the novel, as she stands naked on the beach just before her suicidal plunge, she is identified with the 'bird with a broken wing ... beating the air above, reeling, fluttering, circling disabled down, down to the water' (p. 189), broken psychologically if not physically by the conditions of her world. There also seems an intentional ambiguity about the 'pigeon-house' – the little refuge which Edna rents. In some ways this can be read as a metaphor for her new independence, representing a place where she can be on her own and where she feels she is adding to 'her strength and expansion as an individual' (p. 156). Yet its very nickname (referring to its smallness) suggests a cage, and though it gives Edna freedom it is also the setting for her ultimately unsatisfactory sexual encounters with Alcée Arobin and Robert Lebrun which contribute to her sense of failure. This image too, then, speaks for the paradoxical dichotomies of female experience – here, the conflicting desires for boundless freedom and for the safety of enclosure, the rejection of constraints co-existing with terror of complete autonomy, and the revolutionary spirit undermined by its own awareness of inevitable defeat.

The most important natural image in the book is the sea. It incorporates the standard Freudian implications of sexual awakening and penetration of the unconscious. It is also used as a symbol of female rebirth, not just in terms of the heroine's recognition of her own physicality, but also of her escape from the taboos of land-locked society. Edna's achievement in learning to swim gives her a 'feeling of exultation ... as if some power of significant import had been given her to control the working of her body and her soul ... She wanted to swim far out, where no woman had swum before' (p. 47). At the same time, the image is shot through with implications of extinction and failure. Early on, Edna is lured by the sea's 'seductive odor' (p. 23), as it calls her with a 'sonorous murmur [which] reached her like a loving but imperative entreaty' (p. 24). Even at her moment of aquatic triumph, she experiences terror; in 'reaching out for the unlimited in which to lose herself' she has a sudden panic-ridden 'quick vision of death', seeing the seemingly huge distance between herself and the land as 'a barrier which her unaided strength would never be able to overcome' (p. 48). This scene foreshadows the final pages of the novel where the sea, 'clamoring, murmuring, inviting the soul to wander in the abysses of solitude' (p. 189) impels Edna to take her own life.

The ambiguity of all these images embodies Chopin's attitudes towards female protest. On the one hand, she is more positive than Wharton about the possibilities of womanly achievement, as is indicated by her very different treatment of female creativity. Edna, inspired by Mlle Reisz's musical talent ('the woman, by her divine art, seemed to reach Edna's spirit and set it free', p. 131) herself turns to painting. Taking to heart the artistic credo of the uncompromisingly eccentric spinster (a representation of individualistic and independent womanhood quite absent from *The House of Mirth*) that 'the artist must possess the courageous soul . . . The soul that dares and defies' (p. 106), she works to develop her own talents, the sign of her newly-aroused selfhood. On the other hand, Chopin is clearly uncertain about how – even if – these possibilities may be realised, and her ambivalence is an organic part of her narrative. Uncommitted to Wharton's kind of sombre fatalism, she is more clear-sighted about the ironies of the female condition. For all their apparent rebelliousness, Edna's yearnings for self-expansion are chiefly centred on conventional romantic ideals. Her 'impassioned, newly-awakened being' (p. 76), stirred by her sexual encounters with Arobin, is directed by her feelings for Robert:

> There came over her the acute longing which always summoned into her spiritual vision the presence of the beloved one, overpowering her at once with a sense of the unattainable. (p. 148)

The fact that Robert himself is clearly an inadequate object of

Edna's desires – like Selden, he is cautious, afraid of involvement, and at a crucial time lets down the woman who trusts him – reinforces Chopin's message that despite all its strivings, at this stage and in this environment female aspiration cannot reach beyond traditional patterns of emotional fulfilment (and Mlle Reisz, admirable though she is, is still deficient as a model of womanly enlargement). Edna is finally defeated not only by social pressures, evidenced in Mme Ratignolle's and Robert's conservative attitudes, and by biological tyrannies, but also by personal conventionality which cannot envisage a new life other than in vaguely romantic terms. Chopin is perfectly aware of the limitations of Edna's 'breaking out', and does not, like Wharton, hint at a Utopia of ideal love. She leaves us, rather, with a realistic vision of womanhood which is both pessimistic and hopeful. Edna is at the end still a victim – of herself as much as of her circumstances – yet in choosing to commit suicide she is making the ultimate bid for freedom. Her 'old terror . . . of being unable to regain the shore' (p. 190) finally overcome, she dies for herself, no longer deluded by false appearances, and in control of her own actions.

Of the three novels under discussion, *The Song of the Lark* is the most overtly radical, not only arguing for wider opportunities for the exercise of female energies but portraying a woman who acts out this vision, successfully overcoming the constraints of sexual orthodoxies and finding a fulfilling alternative to the norm of marriage. The heroine, Thea Kronborg, is in part based on the Swedish soprano Olive Fremstad, whom Cather first met in 1913 when gathering material for an article on 'Three American Singers' for *McClure's Magazine*. Fremstad symbolised for Cather the woman artist who single-handedly fights her way to a pinnacle of individual achievement, and her admiration for her is captured in her vigorous depiction of female self-assertion. Cather also put much of herself into her heroine, many of whose opinions and youthful experiences are direct reflections of her own. As this semi-autobiographical portrait makes clear, Cather was more openly rebellious than either Chopin or Wharton. Apparently untroubled by the tensions of conflicting roles and aims which they experienced, she expressed her unconventionality from an early age. She enjoyed considerable freedom as a child in the Nebraska frontier town in which she grew up, resisting those social codes which she found unacceptable. She despised current female fashion, showed a keen interest in scientific research (her High School graduation oration was about vivisection) and at one time wanted to be a surgeon. An entry in a friend's album reveals Cather's determined unorthodoxy: speaking as if a man (she signed herself 'William Cather M.D.'), she noted that she had little toleration for lack of 'nerve', regarded doing fancy-work as 'real misery', and approved of pants and a coat instead of the 'folly' of dresses and skirts.[10] While still at High School, she shocked her friends by dressing as a boy and cutting her hair short, an appearance she maintained during her first year at university; in childhood dramatic productions, she played male parts, and did the same as a student. If much of this, regarded by many people as eccentric, even outrageous behaviour, was merely a deliberately provocative gesture, it nevertheless expressed Cather's real determination to discard traditional notions of feminine roles. Well-educated in science, the classics, and modern languages, she scorned the vacuous and unintellectual existence of most of the women around her, and with single-minded purposefulness worked to achieve her early ambition of being a writer. She never married, enjoying instead close friendships with women (she wrote *The Song of the Lark* at the home of the earliest of these, Isabelle McClung) and, unlike Chopin and Wharton, was professionally self-supporting all her life, as editor, teacher and writer.

Cather's own successful unorthodoxy is the shaping force behind her novel. Thea is both the most unrestricted and the most positively ambitious of the three heroines, with clear views about the kind of path she intends to take. Fired with an almost Promethean spirit of rebellion, she challenges the hostile realities of the outside world which she sees as 'lined up against her' and is determined that the 'something' which is hers shall never be taken from her.[11] In many ways, her background encourages her unconventionality. Though she comes from a male-oriented pioneering family (in the opening chapter, her father's enthusiasm for his new son makes him oblivious to his daughter's sickness), her independent-minded mother is prepared to help her follow a different line from most women, as Cather's own mother did for her. The young Thea can do virtually what she likes; she has a room of her own, roams freely around the town, and visits her friend and mentor, Dr Archie, a married man, alone in his surgery at night. She rejects many of the social and religious mores of her society, and recognises that in order to achieve her goal she must separate herself from their constraining influence; as she leaves Moonstone for Chicago the second time, she determines, 'she was going away to fight and she was going away forever' (p. 246).

Thea's self-dependence also involves rejection of the womanly roles of wifehood and motherhood. Marriage is not part of her plans; her mother astutely comments that 'Thea is not the marrying kind ... I don't see Thea bringing up a family' (p. 102), and the girl herself, watching the Mexican Mrs Tellamantez suffer silently over her crazy, drunken husband, reflects that 'there is nothing so sad in the world as that kind of patience and resignation' (p. 44). Challenging the creed of passive wifely subordination, she refutes the prediction of her first music teacher, Herr Wunsch, that she will marry and become a mere housekeeper; her instinctive reaction to a lightly thrown-out proposal from Fred Ottenburg, her patron and admirer, is that marriage and family life would be 'perfectly hideous', destroying her delight in 'waking up every morning with the feeling that your life is your own, and your strength is your own, and your talent is your own' (p. 317); and later, she indignantly turns down an offer which depends on her buying off her suitor's estranged wife. Thea's dissent from the normality of matrimonial commitment derives partly from her dedication to her own individual development and partly from her urge towards self-preservation. Thea owes much of her success to male intervention in her life: Dr Archie encourages her to take herself seriously; Wunsch inspires her with the notion of becoming the greatest woman singer of her day; the musician, Andor Harsanyi, teaches her that her real talent lies in singing, not in piano-playing; Fred promotes her; and her very career would never have got under way without the assistance of Ray Kennedy, her childhood admirer, who leaves her the money to study in Chicago. But she is much more hard-headed than Lily or Edna about men, who in this novel are seen more as social or economic units than as sources of romantic interest. She regards them as restrictions upon her, despising their attempts to use women and hating the liberties which they take with her. Though they show her the way to freedom, she does not even momentarily find in them the source of that freedom, as Lily does in Selden; Thea, in fact, can flourish only by protecting her inner self from men, so that her relationship with Ray, for example, is attractive to her because 'he never, by any chance, for a single instant, understood her! ... with Ray she was safe; by him she would never be discovered!' (p. 109). Even with Fred, whom she both likes and respects, she is always conscious of the threat of male manipulation; her refusal to accept his offer to pay for her to go to Germany is based on self-consideration as much as on ethics – 'you'd simply be keeping me', she tells him (p. 355). The ambiguity of the word 'keep', which occurs several times in conversations between them, indicates Thea's reservations about masculine patronage. Whereas Fred, by supporting her, thinks he would be able to 'keep her free' (p. 341), for her such 'keeping' implies curtailment of the female personality, as a 'kept' woman (p. 360). Significantly, most of the men in the story are removed by the plot from seriously threatening Thea's expanding individuality: Ray dies; Archie is already married, and when his wife later dies he feels too old to re-marry; Fred, too, turns out to be married, tied to a mental invalid until her death in the closing pages – a commitment his concealment of which does not endear him to Thea.

As with the other two novels, *The Song of the Lark* expresses its ideas about female independence through its use of imagery associated with nature. Thea's rebirth, her awakening to her real needs and goals, takes place in Panther Canyon, Arizona, where, in an environment untouched by modern civilisation and embodying a harmony between nature and the primitive creative spirit, she experiences a kind of apocalyptic vision of a new life. Nature here neither betrays her nor lures her with an ambiguous seductiveness, but becomes part of her inner being, the expression of her selfhood. The key image of the novel is the bird, reminding us once more of *The House of Mirth* and *The Awakening*. Thea is of course linked with the lark of the title, though as Cather herself pointed out in her 1932 Preface, the lark's song does not refer to 'the vocal accomplishments of the heroine', but to a painting about a peasant girl looking up at a singing skylark, suggesting 'a young girl's awakening to something beautiful'.[12] Other bird imagery more appropriately describes the heroine, drawing on traditional associations in contrast to the reversal or duality of meaning of Wharton's and Chopin's. Thus Thea is represented by an untamed, magnificent species. She is not a 'nest-building bird' (p.317) but a 'wild bird ... beat[ing] its passionate wings' (p.187) which, unlike Edna's sea-bird, continues to fly upwards. The central symbol of her aspiration is the eagle, touched by the sun, which she watches flying out of the canyon and which is the literal and metaphorical embodiment of her own high-reaching – 'O eagle of eagles! Endeavor, achievement, desire, glorious striving of human art! From a cleft in the heart of the world she saluted it ...' (p.321). There is no caging here and the striven-for heights do not prove illusory.

Cather's vindication of female self-assertion is assured and powerful in this novel. Thea triumphs in her artistic role as a great singer, and creative talent here is presented unequivocally as alternative womanly fulfilment, the expression of personal autonomy. As a successful career woman, Thea enacts possibilities closed to Lily and only peripherally significant for Edna. Cather does not question the validity of such an achievement, nor suggest that it has failed to answer her heroine's needs. Though, too, she is clear about the price which a woman artist must pay – Thea has no personal life apart from that which derives from her art – and acknowledges the pain and trials involved in such commitment, she conveys no sense of compromise or second-best. Yet there remains a hint of ambivalence at the end of the novel, perhaps more the result of capitulation to literary convention than of Cather's own doubts. We are told in the Epilogue that Thea has married Fred after all. The event is merely briefly reported with reference to its effect on Tillie, Thea's adoring maiden aunt, from whose point of view most of the Epilogue is presented, and it is significant that Cather herself seems to have had second thoughts about it since in her 1937 revisions of the novel she makes even brusquer mention of the marriage.[13] This last-minute suggestion that Thea's self-dependence is not so secure as it seemed and that women do need the fulfilment of conventional sexual relationships is incongruous with the preceding narrative and too undeveloped to make any real point; it provides an unconvincing conclusion to what is otherwise a triumphant portrayal of independent womanhood.

Taken together, then, these three novels show how female writers can articulate their attitudes towards the position of women in their society through the language and patterning of their fiction. The differences between the overall 'messages' of their works indicate their contrasting outlooks; as we have seen, there is a progression from Wharton's not fully acknowledged ambivalence, to Chopin's more honest suggestion of dualities, and finally to Cather's almost complete assurance, which, if it still recognises difficulties in the achievement of female independence, sees these as social and external, rather than cosmic or internal. What they all have in common, though, is the sense that these issues must be faced and that women's resistance to falsifying sexual ideologies must be expressed. In taking the traditional themes of fiction and re-writing them, they are telling us that common assumptions about womanhood are no longer viable; even their ambivalence argues for change.

Notes

1. There is a useful comparative discussion of the feminist movement in England and America in Olive Banks, *Faces of Feminism* (Martin Robertson, Oxford, 1981).
2. These and other details of Wharton's curiously fragmented life can be found in R.W.B. Lewis's excellent study, *Edith Wharton: a Biography* (Constable, London, 1975).
3. Edith Wharton, *The House of Mirth* (Holt, Rinehart & Winston, New York, 1962), p. 11. All subsequent page references are to this edition and will be included in the text.
4. See Lewis, *Edith Wharton*, pp. 65-6, 87, 121 and *passim*.
5. Henry James, *The Portrait of a Lady*, Chapters XII and XXXIV.
6. Lewis, *Edith Wharton*, p. 155. Wharton made this comment in a letter to Sara Norton.
7. See the entry on Chopin in the *Dictionary of American Biography* (Scribner, New York, 1930), Vol. IV, p. 91.
8. *The Complete Works of Kate Chopin*, ed. Per Seyersted (Lousiana State University Press, Baton Rouge, 1969), pp. 24, 17. The Introduction and Preface to this collected edition, from which the two quotations respectively are taken, give a brief account of Chopin's life and literary charac-

teristics. Fuller details are available in Seyersted's *Kate Chopin: A Critical Biography* (Louisiana State University Press, Baton Rouge, 1969).

9. Kate Chopin, *The Awakening* (The Women's Press, London, 1979), p. 53. All subsequent page references are to this edition and will be included in the text.

10. The relevant pages in the album are reproduced in Mildred R. Bennett, *The World of Willa Cather*, new edition (University of Nebraska Press, Lincoln, 1961), pp. 112-13. This work contains much useful information about Cather, but even in its revised edition with notes it is annoyingly disorganised and undocumented. James Woodress's later study, *Willa Cather: Her Life and Art* (University of Nebraska Press, Lincoln, 1970) is fuller and more coherent, though Woodress acknowledges his debt to Bennett in respect of biographical material.

11. Willa Cather, *The Song of the Lark* (1915 edn, Bison Books, Lincoln, Nebraska, 1978), p. 201. All subsequent references are to this edition and will be included in the text.

12. Willa Cather, *The Song of the Lark* (1937 edn, Virago, London, 1980), p. vii.

13. The 1915 version reads, 'When the Denver papers announced that Thea Kronborg had married Frederick Ottenburg, the head of the Brewer's Trust, Moonstone people expected that Tillie's vain-gloriousness would take another form' (p. 484). In the 1937 edition, the reference to the event is so brief and oblique that it might easily be missed; as Tillie reminisces about the time when the Metropolitan Opera came to Kansas City, she reflects on 'the kindness of Mr. Ottenburg! When Thea dined in her own room, her husband went down to dinner with Tillie ... '(p.578).

8

FEMINISM AND FICTION BETWEEN THE WARS: WINIFRED HOLTBY AND *VIRGINIA WOOLF*

Marion Shaw

At the end of *Women* (1934), Winifred Holtby lists twelve of the laws passed in England since women obtained political enfranchisement. These laws were concerned with the rights and protection of women and children and were part of the growth in 'welfarism' in the interwar years. Winifred Holtby saw such reformed administration as a result of the campaigns conducted by enfranchised women: Save the Mothers Campaign, Nursery School Movement, and the National Association for the Prevention of Infant Mortality are some of the examples she gives. Her generation of women, who came to maturity during or just after the war, inherited the legacy of the suffrage movement; they had also survived the war as many of their male peers had not. A complex sense of guilt, of privilege and of responsibility towards the future had made of many of them - Winifred Holtby is an extreme but not untypical example - ceaseless workers for a more just and humane society, in particular for a better world for women. Winifred Holtby's proud list of achievements, and indeed *Women* as a whole, testifies to the harvest that she believed women's enfranchisement has reaped.

Yet in *Women* Holtby arbitrates, with customary but not entirely confident fairness of judgement, between two strands of feminism into which the women's movement was split. It was a split which has continued to the present time. The Equalitarians, as Holtby calls them, who politically were aligned with a Centre/Liberal position, demanded parity with men in rights, treatment and responsibilities. Theirs was a classical feminist position, their most characteristic body was the Six Point Group and their champion was Margaret Rhondda. By contrast, those who called themselves the 'new' feminists and who were largely trade union women like Eleanor Rathbone, were conscious of the special disabilities and requirements of women, particularly in regard to maternity, and sought to legislate for their privileged treatment. That there was hostility between the two feminist factions is evident in Eleanor Rathbone's comments:

> There are two schools of thought, sometimes differentiated as the old and the new feminism. To the minds of the former school, the objective of the movement is still conditioned and limited by the conception of equality between men and women, interpreted in terms of identity: – identity of political and civil rights; identity of occupational opportunities, conditions and remuneration. Whatever in these respects men have got, women must have; and when they have got it, that is equality, and that is the goal of the women's movement.
>
> The new feminists, as we sometimes call ourselves, for frankly I belong to them, scoff at this other school by calling them, in a phrase first coined by Miss Kathleen Courtney, the 'Me too' feminists. Are women, we ask, to behave for ever like a little girl running behind her big brother and calling out, 'Me, too?'[1]

As Eleanor Rathbone pointed out, the divergence of view was particularly marked over the status of women as housewives and mothers, and was crucial to the issue of protective legislation: Must legislation which applies to the adults of one sex only be invariably rejected in the name of equality and irrespective of its merits or whether those to be protected desire it or not? The answer of the 'Me too' school is, 'Yes'. The justification of the 'Me too' position was, in Winifred Holtby's words, that 'special regulations advocated as privilege become disabilities'.

A similar split between privileging women and, on the other hand, assuming their total equality with men can be seen in the literary world. This analogy with the political division should not be strained but its validity is affirmed by a new consciousness, amongst women writers particularly, about what constituted 'women's writing' and whether this could, or should, be distinct from established literary practice. In the aftermath of the war the literary world was dominated by men, in the case of the novel by the 'Edwardians' (Bennett, Wells, Galsworthy) who, though they wrote in a realist tradition, formed at least as much by women as by men, were seen by themselves and by their contemporaries, most obviously Virginia Woolf, as established in a masculinist supremacy of form and style. This was, however, becoming increasingly challenged, even during the pre-war period. In discarding the current 'form of conventionalized human association', Dorothy Richardson saw her alternative choice in 1911 as 'attempting to produce a feminine equivalent of the current masculine realism', what she defined as a 'contemplated reality having for the first time in [my] experience its own say'.[2] When May Sinclair wrote a review of 'The Novels of Dorothy Richardson' in 1918, she described this reality as 'moments tense with vibration, moments drawn out fine, almost to snapping point... There is no drama, no situation, no set scene... It is just life going on and on. It is Miriam's stream of consciousness going on and on.'[3] To May Sinclair, consciousness was 'immediate sense perception, all feeling and willing ... the sudden flash of the instantaneous present ... the stream of thought.'[4] Sinclair's novels, which in this respect resemble Dorothy Richardson's, demonstrate her attempt to convey the 'flash of the instantaneous present' by means of a prose style which mimics the art of perception and in which the associative operations of the mind apparently dictate the choice and order of words:

> She lay on the big bed. Her head rested on Mamma's arm. Mamma's face was close to her. Water trickled into her eyes out of the wet pad of pocket handkerchief. Under the cold pad a hot grinding pain came from the hole in her forehead. Jenny stood by the bed. Her face had waked up and she was busy squeezing something out of a red sponge into a basin of pink water.[5]

Unlike Dorothy Richardson, May Sinclair would not have claimed this as an essentially female style. Her position was more that whatever its sources and whoever else might use it, this was a style peculiarly suited to mapping the largely uncharted territory of women's subjective lives. This was a position similar to Virginia Woolf's. Woolf's reviews (1919 and 1923) of Dorothy Richardson's novels acknowledge their method as a concern with being female, representing 'a genuine conviction of the discrepancy between what she has to say and the form provided by tradition for her to say it in'. She approvingly quotes Miriam's soliloquy on submission to a traditional style: 'there was something wrong, some mannish cleverness that was only half right. To write books knowing all about style would be to become like a man.' What Dorothy Richardson has 'invented', instead of traditional realism, is 'a sentence which one might call the psychological sentence of the feminine gender. It is of a more elastic fibre than the old, capable of stretching to the extreme, of suspending the frailest particles, of enveloping the vaguest shapes.'[6] This attempt to write 'like a woman' is to be applauded; there is, she says in *A Room of One's Own*, 'a highly developed creative faculty among women ... But this creative power differs greatly from the creative power of men ... It should be a thousand pities if women wrote like men ... Ought not education to bring out and fortify the differences rather than the similarities?'[7] But as Michèle Barrett has pointed out,[8] the 'different' style Virginia Woolf notes in Dorothy Richardson, and which she could be described as practising herself, is not seen by her as a biological imperative but rather the result of conscious choice by the woman writer whose 'new' subject matter of 'the psychology of her sex' requires new methods:

> Other writers of the opposite sex have used sentences of this description and stretched them to the extreme. But there is a difference. Miss Richardson has fashioned her sentence consciously, in order that it may descend to the depths and investigate the crannies of Miriam Henderson's consciousness. It is a woman's sentence, but only in the sense that it is used to describe a woman's mind by a writer who is neither proud nor afraid of anything that she may discover in the psychology of her sex.[9]

Whatever the distinctions in thought between Sinclair, Richardson and Woolf concerning how intrinsic to the female gender certain styles of writing may be, their beliefs and practice cohered formidably on the importance to the woman writer of 'the psychology of her sex' and the need for new literary forms – though these may be, as Virginia Woolf put it, 'the spasmodic, the obscure, the fragmentary, the failure' – to express it. What this affirmation, by an already distinguished triumvirate, articulated for other women writers of the post-war period, at least those who were at all alert to the literary scene, was a choice in the way they could write. Not only did they not have to use male pseudonyms to gain respectability, neither did they have to write like men (or, to put it more accurately, to write in the current Edwardian fashion which the male novelists seemed to have stamped as their own) to be taken seriously. This, for the first time, was a real choice; it had always been possible to write 'like a woman' but the great Victorian women novelists had to write and be acclaimed as classics before such a choice could begin to have literary pretensions and its potential be explored. Now also, as Sinclair's and Woolf's filial criticism attested, the question of what it had meant being a woman writer in the Victorian period could be asked, and, more important, what new directions this newly discovered female tradition should take.

Recent feminist criticism, and the recuperative publishing activity accompanying it, has tended to concentrate on those novelists who chose experimentalism and who were most obviously the 'new' feminists of the literary world of the war and interwar years: Woolf, Sinclair, Richardson, Lehmann, Rhys, for example. Less recovered, though well enough known in their own day, are those who chose otherwise, and continued to write 'Edwardian' novels, who, in other words, adhered more or less to the realist traditions of documentary verisimilitude and external or descriptive presentation of character of much nineteenth-century fiction, 'conservative' novelists like Hilda Reid, Naomi Mitchison, Stella Benson, Vera Brittain, Phyllis Bentley and Winifred Holtby. Like their male counterparts, these novelists frequently turned the skills inherited from George Eliot and Elizabeth Gaskell into developing the historical novel (or its familial version, the saga novel) into which they infused considerable erudition and political sagacity and which they often placed in a regional or an exotically remote setting: Phyllis Bentley's *Inheritance* and Naomi Mitchison's *The Corn King and the Spring Queen* are good examples of similar novels very differently located. *Inheritance* (1932) charts the fortunes of a family of textile manufacturers from the time of the Huddersfield Luddites to the present day. Like *Carr*, Phyllis Bentley's favourite novel, *Inheritance*, was intensely researched and written 'in exactly the form of a real biography about a real man, with dates and quotations from letters and diaries and newspapers ... The invention of corroborative detail has always been a delight to me.' Bentley's purpose in writing novels was, she said, to 'present life exactly as it really was, and by so doing help to better the world ... Thus it seemed now to me that the artist's duty was to present life by means of a pattern, so vividly, so convincingly, so interestingly and of course so truthfully, that the reader should ... perceive the season and nature of the thing.'[10] To present life 'as it really was ... truthfully' was, of course, the aim of Richardson, Sinclair and Woolf but in Bentley's case it was a reality conceived in documentation ('the invention of corroborative detail') and through the externality of a historical method. Naomi Mitchison, whose magnificent and prodigiously researched *The Corn King and the Spring Queen* (1931) is set in Sparta and Alexandria between 228 and 187 BC, shared these realist intentions: 'I have tried to deduce a place from a good deal of evidence of actual ideas and happenings in all sorts of other times and places.'[11]

These novelists' interest in history as fiction is easy to understand. The first generation of women to receive university education, most of them had read History which gave them expertise and confidence, yet to be a professional historian must have still seemed out of reach. Moreover, amongst their whole generation there was a need to understand and interpret the past, a need which led women like the war-torn Vera Brittain to turn to a training in History:

such rationality as I still possessed reasserted itself in a desire to understand how the whole calamity had happened, to know why it had been possible for me and my contemporaries, through our own ignorance and others' ingenuity to be used, hypnotised and slaughtered ... Perhaps the careful study of man's past will explain to me much that seems inexplicable in his disconcerting present. Perhaps the means of salvation are already there, implicit in history, unadvertised, carefully concealed by the war-mongers, only awaiting rediscovery to be acknowledged with enthusiasm by all thinking men and women.[12]

Furthermore, as women, to write of the past as fiction cast it within a domestic sphere in ways which complemented, if not usurped the official histories. Historical fiction provided (and still provides) a means by which women could appropriate a past that had largely been denied them. The realist form these women writers chose was peculiarly suitable for their chronicles of the newly learned or imagined details of distant family lives and successions.

In 1931 Winifred Holtby, who reviewed extensively, chose five 'Novels of the Year' for the *Bookman*. The first two novels on her list were *The Corn King and the Spring Queen* and *The Waves*. She is quite aware in her review that the distinction between the two novels is primarily that of form. Although Mitchison's book is about distant civilisations and Woolf's about the present, it is not so much in their choice of action and setting that the difference lies but in the way the characters' lives are presented, by 'a direct, full, varied ... handling of the external show of things' in Mitchison's case and by 'the subconscious monologue, the extreme development of symbolism, and the sustained unity of conception' in Woolf's. With Mitchison 'one simply knows that this is a real world; that real people lived in it; that this is how they lived. These concrete and intimate details of manner, thought and life, the whole external arrangement of three completely different civilizations ... are handled ... as though she were telling us something that had actually happened and that she had seen.' *The Waves*, by contrast, penetrates 'deeper and deeper into a very small, very restricted area ... the regions of human experiences lying outside our bright, busy world of deliberate speech and action'. But although Holtby acknowledges the 'difference' of Woolf's writing, she does not claim in this review that it is peculiarly 'female'.

The next year she published *Virginia Woolf*, her only full-length critical study and the first one in English on Woolf whom she chose as a writer 'whose art seemed most of all removed from anything I could ever attempt, and whose experience was most alien to my own'. Indeed, two more different women living and writing in London at this time could hardly have been found.

The daughter of a Yorkshire farmer and his ex-governess wife, Winifred Holtby went to Somerville College in 1919 where, like Vera Brittain, she read History. This early life and her subsequent career as a single woman actively and cheerfully involved in most of the progressive political movements of her time, distinguish Holtby's experiences and attitudes markedly from the culturally privileged but claustrophobic upbringing of Virginia Woolf and the reclusive semi-invalidism of her later life. (Some of the cultural and class distinctions between the two women are indicated in Woolf's comments on Holtby as 'that enthusiastic and amiable ass [who] learned to read, I'm told, while minding the pigs';[13] although Woolf was perfectly civil and not unhelpful to Holtby during the writing of *Virginia Woolf*.) There were also, as their writings reveal, important differences in their feminism; both wanted an end to the sex war but in Woolf's case what was required was a cooperation – 'when the two live in harmony together, spiritually cooperating' – between the essentially different male and female consciousnesses: 'the difference between the sexes is, happily, one of great profundity'. Holtby could not admit to this difference, or at least could not accept that such a distinction was useful to make; to her the common humanity of men and women should be emphasised, not their separateness: 'we cannot recognize infallibly what characteristics beyond those which are purely physical are "male" and "female". Custom and prejudice, history and tradition have designed [them]: we hardly know yet what remains beneath them of the human being.'[14]

Vera Brittain considered *Virginia Woolf* to be 'the profoundest of Winifred's books' and her estimate is true in so far as the book shows Holtby coming to terms with her own powers and ambitions through a respectful and sympathetic analysis of her opposite. In doing so it develops the distinctions mooted in the *Bookman* review and also, albeit tentatively, considers these distinctions in relation to notions of sexual difference in writing. Modest though it is in its aspirations – Holtby called it an 'essay' – *Virginia Woolf* articulates and summarises the debate occurring amongst women writers at this time, one relating to the crucial issue – then and now – of how separate, privileged and celebrated 'femaleness' could and should be. For Holtby and for women writers in general the issue brought into focus questions concerning their moral and political responsibilities, the accessibility and popularity of their books, and the integrity of their artistic methods.

Holtby was obviously fascinated by the rich contradictions of Woolf's life. *Virginia Woolf* begins with a biographical section, drawn from information supplied to Holtby by Woolf herself, which indicates the divisions Holtby considered important to Woolf's development as a writer. Her style, for instance – 'that peculiar humour, consisting of a mixture of irony and extravagance ... the trick of remote and yet illuminating reference ... the wandering, contemplative mind' was inherited from her mother, Julia Stephens, Holtby suggests, whose pamphlet *Notes from Sick Rooms* she had resourcefully discovered:

> Here, for instance, is a characteristic passage about 'Crumbs in the Bed'. 'Among the number of small evils which haunt illness, the greatest, in the misery which it can cause, is crumbs. The origin of most things has been decided on, but the origin of crumbs in bed has never excited sufficient attention among the scientific world...'
> 'The origin of most things has been decided on.'... Is not that an almost perfect Virginia Woolf remark ...?[15]

At least by implication, then, Woolf's method of writing is established as female but other qualities, particularly her fearlessness as a writer, are seen as valuable inheritances from her father: 'For all her delicacy, sensitiveness and restricted contact with the world, she was intellectually free, candid and unafraid', and this because of the untrammelled intellectual environment provided by her agnostic, truth-seeking father.

Holtby also identified in Woolf's situation a dilemma close to her own, whether to be, as she wrote about herself, 'a reformer-sort-of-person or a writer-sort-of-person'. In Woolf's case, 'the early years of the twentieth century were difficult for a woman who was an artist ... There was the whole movement for the enfranchisement of women. And while on the one hand the suffragettes opened new opportunities and suggested new interests to a woman, at the same time they summoned her to sacrifice the preoccupations of the artist ... Writers ... were torn between their obligations to art and their obligations to society.' But probably most distracting and burdensome of all for women of Woolf's generation (and of course Holtby's own) were the discoveries of psychoanalysis and its obsession with sex and sexual difference. In a passage very revealing of her own position, Holtby protested that at the time when a woman writer

> might have climbed out of the traditional limitations of domestic obligation by claiming to be a human being, she was thrust back into them by the authority of the psychologist... Her impulses, her convictions, every notion that entered her head came to her, somehow or other, from her womanhood. Her sex was all that really mattered about her ... If it were true ... that men and women differed in the physical phenomenon of their sex alone, then, since this physical phenomenon was held to be by far the most important thing about them, it must also be true that their differences were much greater than their likenesses. Their common humanity shrank to a small and unreliable generalization.[16]

The rest of *Virginia Woolf*, which covers all Woolf's work up to and including *The Waves*, develops arguments implicit in this introductory section on her circumstances and attitudes. For instance, Woolf's attack on the Edwardian novelists as 'materialists' is one that occupies Holtby at some length. In the first place it is an inconsistency in Woolf's thought; at times in Woolf's writing 'Marx himself has hardly put the materialistic interpretation of psychology more clearly' yet her attack on the Edwardians' concern 'not with the spirit but with the body' contradicts this and in Holtby's view is untenable: 'For the truth, of course, is that during our mortal life ... absolute and contingent are bound up together ... we are bound in mortality.' Furthermore, Woolf's position appears to represent an artistic elitism and an abnegation of ethical responsibility that is unacceptable to Holtby; it jeopardises the compromise between reformer-sort-of-person and writer-sort of-person that Holtby strove for:

> One of [Woolf's] complaints against the Edwardians was that their novels were not ends in themselves. 'In order to complete them it seems necessary to do something – to join a Society or, more desperately, to write a cheque' ... but she could not disguise even

from herself the fact that though art may be, theoretically, an 'end in itself', it concerns morality ... A work of art is not destroyed because its secondary influence upon those who encounter it is moral and persuasive. Galsworthy's play *Justice* does not fail because it has driven stall-holders to sign cheques for the Howard League of Penal Reform.[17]

These arguments coalesce round the issue of Woolf's feminism in the chapter called 'Two in a Taxi' which is mainly concerned with *Orlando* and *A Room of One's Own*. Having described and admired Woolf's mature technique in *Mrs Dalloway* and *To The Lighthouse*, Holtby now draws her conclusions in relation to Woolf's views on the differing creativity of men and women. She acknowledges that Woolf's ideal is a 'human communism of intellectual experience', the androgynous mind represented by the taxi ride in *A Room of One's Own*. But this state is not one of hermaphroditism; reality would still be apprehended through a psychological condition of being male or female. And it is here that Holtby suspects the error in Woolf's thinking of the notion of an irreducible maleness or femaleness, an essence of each which in psychological terms is unaltered by altered material conditions. Holtby's hope is that so fundamental a division does not exist; more realistically, she believes that one cannot *know* that it does exist and that it is restrictive and unprogressive to assume it does:

> looking round upon the world of human beings as we know it, we are hard put to it to say what is the natural shape of men or women, so old, so all-enveloping are the moulds fitted by history and custom over their personalities. We do not know how much of sensitiveness, intuition, protectiveness, docility and tenderness may not be naturally "male", how much of curiosity, aggression, audacity and combativeness may not be "female" ... The time has not yet come when we can say for certain which is the man and which the woman, after both have boarded the taxi of human personality ...[18]

To some extent, Holtby misunderstood Woolf's views, particularly those on whether a certain style of writing is intrinsically female rather than adopted by women as suited to their subject-matter. But if this had been clear to her, it is unlikely she

185

would have accepted, for her own part, even this degree of separateness. As it is, to Holtby, Woolf's apparent assumption of an essential femaleness which has a special creativeness to be fostered and expressed through feminine forms of fiction is a political weakness in her theoretical arguments in *A Room* and perhaps also in her practice in her novels which, though they strive towards 'a humanity stronger in its spiritual unity than in its sexual difference', are nevertheless, because of the way they are written and the aesthetic their author has chosen, limited: 'the immense detailed knowledge of the material circumstances of life ... is beyond her. She will remain ... shut off from intimate contact with Hilda Thomas of Putney and Edgar J. Watkiss, who lays lead piping among the bowels of Bond Street.' What Holtby fears is that the refinement, interiority and introspection of what she perceives as a feminine aesthetic may result in a gender-bound, class-bound uselessness and passivity. In Holtby's view, literature should be an agent of change; it should address itself to the social conditions of its time, it should help to write history, not in any crude programmatic way but by careful analysis of 'the material circumstances of life' which are the preconditions not only of how people live but of the consciousness which informs their life-style. Literature can best fulfil these responsibilities by eschewing the kind of feminism Holtby believes Woolf represents.

The final chapter of *Virginia Woolf* is on *The Waves*, 'the most delicate, complex and aesthetically pure piece of writing that [Woolf] has yet produced', and the one that evokes Holtby's most equivocal response. Although she admires the novel as 'extraordinarily rich in texture', it nevertheless represents a limitation and a possible ending. For there are in Woolf, Holtby suggests, returning to the notion of her divided literary inheritance, 'two streams of thought': 'one practical, controversial, analytical; the other creative, poetical, audacious'. From the evidence of *The Waves*, Holtby's prediction is that these contradictory impulses will continue to develop separately: 'her novels will grow more subtle and intricate as her criticism grows more orderly, stiffened perhaps into some kind of system.' More than the previous novels, *The Waves* has withdrawn from the world of contingent reality; its effect is 'an extraordinary [Holtby uses this word repeatedly of *The Waves*] transparency and fluidity...

as though human life were already melted into a watery universe'; in particular, its use of sea symbolism is excessive and irrelevant, 'quite unrelated to the history of her characters'. In such writing there is no place for humour, satire and 'the trappings of flesh and bone, surnames, positions and continuous narrative', or any of the insights and analyses of the social commentator and historian-narrator. What is disturbing about *The Waves* is that it represents a denial of the analytical and political qualities of its author's mind; these qualities have been relegated to her non-fiction polemic. In this *The Waves* betrays what Holtby undoubtedly viewed as the moral and social responsibilities of fiction, its role as what George Eliot would have called an 'aesthetic teacher'. If in doing this, *The Waves* privileges the 'feminine' by its intense subjectivism and by the way it is written, then to Holtby this was too costly an exercise in terms of the loss of a common humanity and a social apprehension of human experience.

Winifred Holtby wrote six novels. In her final novel, *South Riding* (1936), begun as she was completing *Virginia Woolf* and written during the last eighteen months of her life, she turned to the form and conventions of nineteenth-century realism with a thoroughness that is almost parody. After her scrutiny in *Virginia Woolf* of a writer whose purpose and manner were so different from her own, she affirmed her allegiance in this novel to a traditional form of writing. Her intentions in writing it were quite clear: to write a popular, that is a familiar and accessible, book whose meaning and teaching could be assimilated by many; to write comprehensively about a whole society across a spectrum of classes and occupations; like her friend Phyllis Bentley, to provide a wealth of corroborative detail relating to 'the material circumstances of life' in the belief that these constitute 'reality' for most people; to make her writing historical in that it should reveal the connections and contradictions between past and future using as a focus an actual historical event of importance to the lives of ordinary people (the 1933 Local Government Act, which of course is reminiscent of George Eliot's use of the 1832 Reform Act in *Middlemarch*); and to propound a moral theme embracing the various stories in the novel, namely the interconnectedness of individuals within society, the need to recognise that 'we are not only single

187

individuals, each face to face with eternity and our separate spirits; we are members one of another'.[19] In the context of Holtby's conclusions in *Virginia Woolf*, this catalogue of motives, and *South Riding* itself, can be seen as a rejoinder to the 'new' literary feminism Woolf seemed to represent.

South Riding won the James Tait Black Memorial Prize in 1937 and has been continuously in print ever since it was first published. It was made into a television serial by Yorkshire Television in 1975. It has kept a steady popularity of a voluntary nature (it is rarely taught in schools and universities) for nearly fifty years which perhaps qualifies it as a classic of its kind. It was deliberately written in classic vein and appeared even in 1936 as a familiar and rather old-fashioned kind of novel.

The question raised by this conscious decision to write in what for a woman novelist at this time can be seen as an anachronistic manner is that of whether it represents a retreat from feminism. Winifred Holtby would have stoutly claimed that it didn't, because of the example of its heroine and because its scope and method proclaim the energy, intelligence and political competence a woman writer can command. Its heroine, Sarah Burton, like Holtby herself, is strong and independent with an idealistic feminism which finds its outlet in teaching. As Muriel Spark says, 'there were legions of her kind during the 1930s ... women from the age of thirty and upward, who crowded their war-bereaved spinsterhood with voyages of discovery into new ideas and energetic practices in art or social welfare, education or religion. [They were] great talkers and feminists and, like most feminists, they talked to men as man-to-man.'[20] What Sarah Burton and her older counterpart Alderman Mrs Beddows are concerned with is the battle against 'our common enemies – poverty, sickness, ignorance, isolation, mental derangement and social maladjustment', which in the precise terms of the novel become the provision of new roads and houses, a maternity clinic and mental hospital, and higher education for a bright working-class girl. These were such important and pressing issues, particularly for women, that to write about them obscurely or in unfamiliar terms would have been contrary to Holtby's democratic and reformist purposes, her own definitions of what being a feminist and socialist meant.

There is also Sarah Burton's staunch spinsterhood. Although

she falls in love, at the end of the novel she is alone, still combative, socially committed and rejoicing in her life, as are all Holtby's heroines whose quest for freedom and adventure, and the cost entailed, is a theme in each of her novels. Women were in excess of men by 1½ million in 1936 and Holtby's feminism in her novels takes the form of showing singleness as a genuine alternative to marriage not merely its unfortunate second-best. When Virginia Woolf wrote, 'Now if Chloe likes Olivia and they share a laboratory ... then I think that something of great importance has happened',[21] she was unwittingly describing the work-and-friendship ethic that Holtby's novels exemplify. By contrast the more experimental work of the 'new' literary feminists – Richardson, Rhys, Lehmann, for instance – seems invariably pessimistic in its depiction of heroines who are vulnerable, dependent, forsaken and self-absorbed.

Holtby was a committed but reluctant feminist, resenting the divisions feminism wrought and its threat to the ideal of a common humanity she held to:

> I am a feminist because I dislike everything that feminism implies. I desire an end of the whole business, the demands for equality, the suggestions of sex warfare, the very name of feminist ... But while inequality exists, while injustice is done and opportunity denied to the great majority of women, I shall have to be a feminist with the motto Equality First.[22]

Equality First was the motto of the Six Point Group which Holtby belonged to. The brisk and uncompromising humanism of this group is expressed through Sarah Burton, who

> believed in action. She believed in fighting. She had unlimited confidence in the power of the human intelligence and will to achieve order, happiness, health and wisdom. It was her business to equip the young women entrusted to her by a still inadequately enlightened state for their part in that achievement. She wished to prepare their minds, to train their bodies, and to inculcate their spirits with some of her own courage, optimism and unstaled delight.[23]

The style here and throughout *South Riding* is equally uncompromising in its unpretentiousness and its near-journalistic

189

concern with information and comment summarily expressed. Whether Holtby is describing characters, events or landscape, she assumes a central view which is as generally and impartially human (rather than male or female) as tradition, usage and the techniques of nineteenth century realism can make it. Her writer's philosophy is of a piece with her political philosophy; as a pacifist and a socialist, and a feminist only by default, it is what unites human beings that is firstly important and only secondly their differences, including their gender. To her, the threat from the 'new' feminist novelists, as from the 'new' feminists like Eleanor Rathbone, was that gender would usurp humanity as a primary condition.

Notes

1. Eleanor Rathbone, 'Changes in Public Life', *Our Freedom and its Results*, ed. Ray Strachey (Hogarth, London, 1936) p. 57.
2. Dorothy Richardson, *Pilgrimage* (1938) (J. M. Dent & Sons, London, 1967), Foreword.
3. May Sinclair, 'The Novels of Dorothy Richardson', *The Egoist*, April 1918, quoted John Rosenberg, *Dorothy Richardson: The Genius They Forgot* (Duckworth, London, 1973), p. 90.
4. May Sinclair, *Proceedings of the Aristotelian Society* (1923) quoted T. E. M. Boll, *Miss May Sinclair: Novelist* (Fairleigh Dickinson University Press, New Jersey, 1973), p. 306.
5. May Sinclair, *Mary Olivier: A Life* (1919) (Virago, London, 1980), p. 15.
6. Virginia Woolf, reviews of Dorothy Richardson's novels, reprinted in *Virginia Woolf: Women and Writing*, ed. Michèle Barrett (The Women's Press, London, 1979), p. 189.
7. Virginia Woolf, *A Room of One's Own* (1928) (Penguin, London, 1945), pp. 86-7.
8. Barrett (ed.), p. 26.
9. Ibid., p. 191.
10. Phyllis Bentley, *'O Dreams, O Destinations': An Autobiography* (Victor Gollancz, London, 1962), pp. 107, 149-50.
11. Naomi Mitchison, *The Corn King and the Spring Queen* (1931) (Virago, London, 1984), Foreword.
12. Vera Brittain, *Testament of Youth* (1933) (Gollancz, London, 1943), p. 332.
13. Letters to Ethel Smyth and Hugh Walpole, *The Letters of Virginia Woolf*, ed. Nigel Nicolson, Vol. v (The Hogarth Press, London, 1979), pp. 114, 250.

14. Winifred Holtby, *Virginia Woolf* (Wishart & Co, London, 1932), pp. 182-3.
15. Ibid., p. 13.
16. Ibid., pp. 27-9
17. Ibid., pp. 44-9.
18. Ibid., p. 183.
19. Winifred Holtby, *South Riding* (1936) (Fontana Books, London, 1954), Prefatory letter to Alderman Mrs Holtby.
20. Muriel Spark, *The Prime of Miss Jean Brodie* (1961) (Penguin, London, 1965), p. 42.
21. Virginia Woolf, *A Room of One's Own* (1928) (Penguin, London, 1945), p. 83.
22. Quoted Vera Brittain, *Testament of Friendship* (1940) (Virago, London, 1980), p. 134.
23. Holtby, *South Riding*, p. 66.

INDEX

Index

193

Index